Don't Go Back to Where You Came from

TIM SOUTPHOMMASANE is a lecturer at Monash University's National Centre for Australian Studies and a research fellow at Per Capita, a public policy think tank. He is also a columnist with *The Age* in Melbourne, a member of the Australian Multicultural Council, and a director of the National Australia Day Council. A first-generation Australian, Tim completed his doctorate in political philosophy at the University of Oxford. His previous books include *Reclaiming Patriotism* and *The Virtuous Citizen*.

Don't GO BACK to WHERE YOU CAME FROM

Why multiculturalism works

TIM SOUTPHOMMASANE

NEWSOUTH

For Sarah

A NewSouth book

Published by
NewSouth Publishing
University of New South Wales Press Ltd
University of New South Wales
Sydney NSW 2052
AUSTRALIA
newsouthpublishing.com

© Tim Soutphommasane 2012
First published 2012

10 9 8 7 6 5 4 3 2 1

National Library of Australia Cataloguing-in-Publication entry
   Author: Soutphommasane, Tim.
     Title: Don't go back to where you came from: why multiculturalism works/Tim Soutphommasane.
     ISBN: 9781742233369 (pbk)
         9781742241203 (epub)
         9781742243788 (mobipocket)
         9781742246109 (epdf)
     Subjects: Multiculturalism – Australia.
       Cultural pluralism – Australia.
     Dewey Number: 305.800994

Design Josephine Pajor-Markus
Cover design Xou Creative
Cover images Thinkstock
Printer Griffin Press

This book is printed on paper using fibre supplied from plantation or sustainably managed forests.

Contents

Introduction

Mention multiculturalism and veils, and one naturally thinks of the controversies that have raged over burqas and hijabs. Yet it was through a very different kind of veil that I was introduced to debates about multiculturalism in the late 1990s. At the time, Pauline Hanson was at the peak of her popularity, leading her One Nation Party's crusade against Asian immigration, multiculturalism and political correctness. During lunchtimes at high school I found myself in debates with students and teachers about whether Hanson was racist, whether she was right about the country being swamped by Asians. There were a good number of teenaged Hansonites among my fellow students. Occasionally someone in class would express their admiration for Hanson, or their disdain for 'gooks' and 'coons'. With my interest in politics awakened, I began reading about multiculturalism and came to be introduced to the 'veil of ignorance'.

The idea was conceived by American political philosopher John Rawls. In his classic *A Theory of Justice*, Rawls famously proposed that we could imagine a hypothetical social contract in a liberal society by placing ourselves behind a veil of ignorance. Imagine we didn't know about our sex, ethnicity, race or religious affiliation. Imagine we didn't know anything about the social position of the families into which we were born. Imagine then trying to agree upon some principles according to which society should be organised. And, finally, imagine being bound by these principles once you stepped from behind the veil and discovered your social identity. According to Rawls, constructing a just society requires us first to put ourselves in this 'original position'. Lest we leave the original position only to discover we were individuals with socially disadvantaged identities, we would want society to offer equal opportunity to all, not to mention limit its inequality. We would want some guarantee of social justice.[1]

As imaginary devices, the original position and veil of ignorance aid in clarifying the nature of our concern with multiculturalism. They remind us what is at stake. How we deal with cultural diversity is far from a marginal affair, relevant only to newly arrived minorities. Just how we conduct our disagreements about matters of integration, immigration and nationhood says a lot about the state of our society. Multiculturalism requires us to confront the matter of social justice – to reflect upon how we collectively live up to ideals of fairness and equality. Too often we celebrate our diversity without first asking whether a fair go and egalitarianism extend to all Australians, regardless of their cultural backgrounds. Too often we are guilty of complacency. What, for example, might have been the case had the gook-baiting, coon-hating Hansonites among my old classmates paused to imagine themselves trapped in the body of an Asian or Aboriginal? What if they had placed themselves in the original position? And what point of view would today's critics of multiculturalism adopt if they weren't to know whether they would find themselves to be Muslims once they stepped out of the original position?

The purpose of this book is to lift a different veil of ignorance. In recent years, it has been hard to find multiculturalism discussed in anything but negative terms. The years of the conservative Howard government, and a resurgent Australian nationalism, seemed to quash enthusiasm for cultural diversity.[2] If anything, the international zeitgeist appeared to confirm that it was time to move on. There is apparent consensus that multiculturalism in Europe has failed to prevent Muslim minorities from becoming, in the words of political scientist Francis Fukuyama, 'a ticking cultural time bomb'.[3] Across Western Europe, successive governments have embraced more muscular, assimilationist policies. For example, in October 2010 German Chancellor Angela Merkel declared that 'Multiculturalism is dead', amid calls from some German politicians for a halt to immigration from Turkey and the Middle East. Not long after, in early 2011, British Prime Minister David Cameron joined in repudiating 'a state doctrine of multiculturalism', as did the then French President Nicolas Sarkozy.

Such developments have emboldened many local commentators and politicians to suggest that Australian governments should do the same.

Yet there are signs of multicultural renewal underway in Australia. In 2011, Minister for Immigration and Citizenship Chris Bowen extolled 'the genius of Australian multiculturalism'.[4] In February 2012, a cabinet reshuffle included the reinstatement of a Commonwealth Minister for Multicultural Affairs. If there has been any crisis of Australian multiculturalism, it has been intellectual, one manufactured by critics. Unlike Europe, high unemployment across generations and regular street riots aren't the characteristic experience of Australian immigrant populations – quite the opposite. After all, it is the sons and daughters of immigrants who dominate enrolments in the law and medicine faculties of our leading universities. Unruly minorities haven't been the ones responsible for the worst of recent rioting, as the 2005 episode at Cronulla reminds us. Even so, many Australians regard the concept of multiculturalism with suspicion. It is associated with a form of social engineering which elevates the value of immigrant cultures over those of traditional, mainstream Australia. Contemporary debates about racism, population growth and asylum seekers suggest that Australians are still grappling with how to negotiate cultural diversity and its challenges. 'Less than a decade ago,' political theorist Geoffrey Brahm Levey wrote in 2011, 'multiculturalism looked to be secure and to have won the day'.[5] Much has since changed.

It is strange that so many are hostile towards multiculturalism. As I will argue, there is every reason to believe there is a good story to be told about it. We have forged a model of cultural diversity that has been a success, by all objective measures. Amid all the talk about multicultural failures across Western liberal democracies, Australia has proven itself to be an exception. The problem is that we've allowed ourselves to forget the distinctive qualities of the Australian experience. Critics of multiculturalism construct straw men and wrongly extrapolate from troubles overseas. Its supporters, meanwhile, rest their case on the ornamental qualities of diversity. Progressive liberals, in particular, embrace the supposed sophistication of cosmopolitan lifestyles. A multicultural Australia has been reduced to the novelty of being able to eat a different ethnic food each day of the week.

This book avoids taking a lifestyle approach to multiculturalism. Cultural diversity isn't only about the range of available cuisines. When we suggest that it is, we can struggle to articulate any deeper significance to culture than food. Such superficiality encourages people to dismiss multicultural policies as mere 'symbolism' or 'gesture politics'. Focusing on lifestyle can mean that we fail to recognise the *civic* dimensions of diversity. We can lose sight of how diversity demands of us answers not only about culture, but about justice and citizenship.

It is important, moreover, to be unapologetic about

the word 'multiculturalism'. Many frequently believe that it evokes a bygone phase of Australian national development.[6] One temptation has been to qualify or even discard the terminology. It may be one thing to refer to the reality of a society composed of people from many ethnic and cultural backgrounds, yet another thing to refer to public policies recognising cultural diversity in a society. It is this second version of multiculturalism – its philosophical or public policy sense – that is the more controversial one. For some, such as former Prime Minister John Howard, there is no issue with referring to a 'multiethnic' or 'multiracial' society, but to speak of 'multiculturalism' in Australia is a different matter.[7] One may accept or tolerate diversity without also wishing to endorse it through government policy.

The word 'multiculturalism' can admittedly mean different things to different people. It could be regarded as an example of an 'essentially contested concept', a word whose meaning is subject to perennial dispute.[8] Whereas conservatives tend to regard it as a form of cultural relativism, progressives tend to view it as a corrective to outmoded views about assimilating immigrants into a majority culture. Even then multiculturalism can defy easy categorisation. There would be some conservatives, for example, who would sympathise with the multicultural impulse to ensure that individuals are free to express their allegiances to their traditional cultures. Some social democrats who believe in a strong welfare state demur that recognising cultural differences may come at the expense of economic redistribution. Some progressive liberals, believing in the ultimate value of individual liberty, have a different objection: that valuing cultural diversity in the form of group identities may be destructive of personal choice and autonomy. Whichever way one turns, there is disagreement. Little wonder the word may appear so confusing and unattractive.

Of course, imprecision or vagueness aren't on their own a valid reason for giving up on a word. If that were the case, we might as well not talk about justice or liberty or equality or democracy. If there is such endless debate about a concept, it is probably because it is an important one. The burden for anyone who invokes multiculturalism, then, isn't to define it in a way that strips it of all controversy. But there must be an effort to avoid laziness and indifference. If we write into multiculturalism our ideological assumptions, as we inevitably do, we should at least acknowledge them.

In this book, multiculturalism will be used in both its sociological sense and its philosophical one. This is for two reasons: first, any social reality of cultural diversity seems to be hollow without there also being a public policy of multiculturalism. Where a society doesn't endorse diversity in some measure, it is likely to fall short on the measures of justice and citizenship. Prejudice, bigotry and racism thrive in the absence of public policies that affirm the freedom of citizens to express their different cultural identities. Second, there has in fact been considerable clarity to the meaning of Australian multiculturalism, which only rarely is acknowledged. As it has existed in policy terms, Australian multiculturalism has been an expression of liberal citizenship and an exercise in nation-building. Cultural diversity goes together with individual liberty: everyone should have a right to express their cultural heritage and identity. This comes, though, with the territory of citizenship. All citizens, whatever their cultural background and beliefs, have a duty to abide by the civic values of an Australian liberal democracy. Far from radical, multiculturalism stands for the proposition that Australian citizenship doesn't rule out being able to have some cultural identification as Italian or Chinese or Lebanese, and so on.

I don't claim in this book to offer a disinterested treatment of our political and cultural debates. My aim is to offer a defence of multiculturalism that is grounded in liberal political philosophy. But while principles are important, they shouldn't be divorced from reality. I begin, therefore, in Chapter 1 with a brief history of Australian multiculturalism, exploring political and policy developments from the early 1970s through to the present. The advent of a culturally diverse society has been accompanied over the past four decades by an official multiculturalism – a policy that has itself evolved through a number of distinct stages. In Chapter 2, I explore the contemporary debate about diversity, including the recent retreat from 'the M word'. I examine the theoretical foundations of Australian multicultural-ism and compare it to other models of integration that exist in Western liberal democracies. Chapter 3 evalu-ates the performance of the Australian model: to what extent do racism and minority under-representation exist in politics, government, the workplace and the media? The following two chapters examine the heated debates about population growth and immigration (Chapter 4), and about asylum seekers and refugees (Chapter 5). While these issues aren't always considered in discus-sions about integration and identity, they arguably rep-resent the greatest potential challenges to a multicultural Australia. Not enough has been said about whether sup-port for multiculturalism requires support for a bigger Australia, and about the impact on social cohesion of public hostility to population growth. There is also the danger that hysteria about asylum seekers may contami-nate public attitudes towards immigration and diver-sity, if it hasn't already. I conclude with some reflections about the future directions for multiculturalism, with special attention to 'the Asian century'. To date, much of the renewed discussion of Australia's place in Asia has focused on the economics of our relationship with the region. Yet it might be in another realm – the cultural – that the most profound challenges of 'the Asian century' lie. It might just be the Australian multicultural experi-ence that will offer us the best guidance.

1

The life and times of multiculturalism

The precise time of multiculturalism's birth is open to debate. Some would say that pluralism has always been present in Australia, given the original presence of some 700 indigenous nations, speaking more than 250 languages – all long before the arrival of the British. Others highlight that the First Fleet included soldiers, sailors and convicts with ancestral origins in Europe, Africa and the Middle East. Others, meanwhile, note that the goldfields of the 19th century were something of a cultural laboratory, populated as they were by diggers from a multitude of nationalities. Yet few would seriously dispute that cultural diversity, at least as we know it today, is the distinctive creation of the second half of the 20th century. Our multicultural society is a product of the successive waves of mass immigration following the Second World War, which have brought more than 7 million people to settle in this country.

And if by multiculturalism we mean a form of government policy responding to ethnic and cultural minorities, there is little ambiguity about the moment of its introduction. Its arrival was modest, the details largely unknown to most Australians. But the first official use of the word 'multicultural' in August 1973 would signify the arrival of a revolution – not one of the sort identified with coups or wars, but of that species that Donald Horne called 'revolutions in consciousness'.[1] It came in a speech delivered by Al Grassby, the then Minister for Immigration in the Whitlam Labor government. 'A multicultural society for the future', as the speech was titled, offered a contemplation of what Australia would look like by the year 2000.[2] The composition of the Australian population, Grassby noted, would be much different as a result of mass immigration. Increasing diversity had 'gradually eroded and finally rendered untenable any prospects there might have been twenty years ago of fully assimilating newcomers to the "Australian way of life"'. It was time to enlarge our understanding of the national identity to reflect the cultural and social impact of Australia's new arrivals:

Our prime task at this point in our history must be to encourage practical forms of social interaction in our community. This implies the creation of a truly just society in which all components can enjoy freedom to make their own distinctive contribution to the family of the nation. In the interests of the Australians of the year 2000, we need to appreciate and preserve all those diverse elements which find a place in the nation today.[3]

For Grassby, the goal was to ensure that Australians of all backgrounds would always be proud to declare, in their different accents, 'I am Australian' – just as Roman citizens in ancient times could boast 'Civis Romanus sum'.

It has often been remarked that Grassby was the father of Australian multiculturalism. Born to an Irish mother and a Spanish father, he was a man whose penchant for flamboyant ties and garish outfits seemed to symbolise the loud, unapologetic insertion of colour into a monochrome Australian society. His intervention in 1973 was certainly a seminal act. According to sociologist Jean Martin, one of the early chroniclers of 'the migrant presence', Grassby's statement was 'a comprehensive document' and 'a manifesto for the plural society' which Grassby was to promote as Minister for Immigration.[4] At the very least, it offered a new language for discussing national identity, and a new perspective on the place of immigrants in Australian society. It acknowledged that a multicultural society was a reality that demanded a national response.

Almost four decades have since passed. What was then a fledgling reality has come to be accepted as a permanent feature of Australian life. As for the response, multiculturalism has evolved through a number of phases since 1973, reflecting not only changes in Australian society but also in political leadership. The story of Australian multiculturalism is one of champions and critics; perhaps even of heroes and villains. But in order to understand it, we must first turn to what preceded it.

After assimilation

Looking back, it isn't hard to see how large-scale assisted immigration – instigated by Ben Chifley's postwar Labor government and continued under that of his Liberal successor Robert Menzies – was bound to transform Australia. It wasn't that the country hadn't experienced waves of immigration before. The gold rush saw Australia's population double in the decade from 1850 to 1860. More than 800000 immigrants from Britain arrived through assisted passage from 1831 to 1900, many seeking prosperity in the 'long boom' that culminated in the 1880s. But from the Depression of the 1890s through to the Second World War period, immigration was limited and the demand for labour low. When the postwar immigration program began in 1947, fewer than 10 per cent of Australians were born overseas. This would change in the decades that followed. Between 1947 and 1964, more immigrants arrived than in the 80 years from 1860.[5] The national population from 1947 to 1973 increased by close to 6 million. Far from being overwhelmingly

British in origin, immigrants came increasingly from central and southern Europe. Diversity had arrived.

The national consciousness was slow to incorporate this new development. At the time, the postwar immigration program was regarded as an imperative born of postwar reconstruction and the strategic requirement of 'populate or perish'. The Department of Immigration, established in 1945 under the watch of its inaugural Minister Arthur Calwell, began planning for the most extensive period of organised migration since convict settlement. A 'scientifically calculated' absorption rate of 70 000 per year was set, aimed at providing a mobile reserve army of labour to meet the demands of an expanding national economy.[6] The grand Snowy Mountains Scheme, designed to generate cheap hydroelectricity for Canberra and elsewhere, captured the public imagination. Here, most literally, was mass immigration as an exercise in building the nation.

Postwar leaders and their bureaucratic planners had no intention of using immigration to remake an Australian identity. For Calwell, in 1946, the preferred source of immigrants was clear: 'Australia hopes that for every foreign migrant there will be ten people from the United Kingdom.'[7] It was only when Britons couldn't be persuaded to come in the numbers required that Australian governments turned to recruiting immigrants from the European continent. This began in 1947 with the Displaced Persons Scheme, which would bring thousands of refugees from Hungary, Czechoslovakia, Poland, Ukraine and the Baltic states. Even then, the non-British nature of such a program wasn't intended to weaken a white Australia. But by the mid-1960s, the mix of arriving immigrants was changing: there were fewer coming from Britain and northern Europe, and an increasing number from southern Europe. Greeks, Italians, Maltese, Lebanese, Spaniards and Yugoslavs made up two-thirds of the migrants from outside the British Isles in 1964. 'The central dilemma of Australian immigration', as immigration scholar James Jupp anticipated in 1966, 'is that the nationalities least likely to assimilate or be accepted are those most likely to come and least likely to leave'.[8]

In theory, the path for any newly arrived immigrant was clearly paved: it was one of assimilation. Immigrants were to discard their cultural baggage – their old languages, customs, attitudes – without delay. They were 'New Australians', who were expected to become indistinguishable from the rest of the Anglo-Celtic population. In practice, assimilation was far from a smooth path. In order to foster conformity to an Australian 'way of life', immigrants were discouraged from forming clubs and organisations based around their ethnicity or cultures. Many immigrants changed their surnames to sound more 'Australian'. It was common for immigrants to be scolded by passers-by for speaking a language other than English in public; children of immigrants suffered the daily embarrassment of being teased for having strange foods for lunch. The experience of assimilation was far from pleasant for many immigrants.[9]

Racial and cultural homogeneity remained a defining principle of nationhood well into the 1960s. The dictum of 'populate or perish' didn't extend to taking in non-Europeans, particularly Asians. Politicians such as Calwell emphasised the desirability of Nordic or Anglo-Saxon racial characteristics among new arrivals. Baltic refugees with blond hair and blue eyes would be welcomed as immigrants who were racially acceptable and ready to be assimilated. Asians and blacks were still commonly regarded as not fit to become members of the Australian nation. 'Two Wongs', as Calwell famously quipped, 'do not make a White'.[10] While the most infamous manifestation of the White Australia policy, the dictation test, was abolished in 1958, even as late as the 1960s immigration officers enjoyed the discretion to turn back applicants for admission, based on their racial appearance.[11]

The ideal of assimilation was accepted by both sides of politics, for it had an obvious appeal. It meant that, '[w]ith one magic stroke, as it were, Australia's economic interests would be served and the resourceful, the needy and the victims of war in Europe be given the chance for a new life, while the continuity of our cultural identity would still be guaranteed'.[12] Certainly, assimilationist ideas helped to sooth anxieties about the destabilising effects of mass immigration. It is perhaps telling that the comic autobiography *They're a Weird Mob* (1957), written by Nino Culotta, proved to be one of the notable literary successes of the 1950s. Later turned into a film in 1966, *They're a Weird Mob* told the story of its author's attempts as a newly arrived Italian immigrant to learn the ways of Australian culture.

Part of the popular appeal of the book – which by 1971 had been reprinted in 50 editions and had sold more than 500 000 copies – no doubt lay in Nino's gradual yet earnest conversion to what he would call 'the informality of the Australian way of life, and the Australian's unquenchable energy and thirst'.[13] The story was a celebratory tale of Australian assimilation, calming people's uncertainty or misgivings about non-Anglo immigration.[14] The moral of the story: postwar immigration was bringing to the country people not necessarily familiar with Australian ways, but most would in time assimilate. As for what immigrants would be assimilating into, it was as much an Australian character as it was an Australian way of life. Assimilation would ensure no threat to the authentically direct, egalitarian, knockabout Australian. For Nino, 'the grumbling, growling, cursing, profane, laughing, beer drinking, abusive loyal-to-his-mates Australian is one of the few free men left on this earth'.[15] Nino had no intention of challenging that ethos. Of course, *They're a Weird Mob* was a work of fiction: 'Nino Culotta' was a pseudonym for Sydney writer John O'Grady.

In reality, assimilation became harder to justify as the guiding principle of immigrant settlement. The dilemma Jupp had identified grew ever more acute during the 1960s. By 1970 an economic boom in Europe meant there were fewer new immigrants from preferred source countries, particularly in northern Europe. There were clear signs that assimilation wasn't working: the rate at which immigrants were returning home climbed sharply in the early 1960s.[16] Those immigrants who did remain were still speaking their languages, still mixing with their old compatriots. Ethnic neighbourhoods and communities were appearing in the capital cities. With the ideal of assimilation crumbling, a new official language of 'integration' emerged.[17] But this was only transitional. Assimilation had run its course, and it would be Grassby's multicultural approach that would take its place.

The shift from assimilation to multiculturalism wasn't peculiar to Australia. Indeed, the concept of multiculturalism had its provenance in North America, where it became Canadian government policy in 1971. Offering the first definition of multiculturalism, Prime Minister Pierre Trudeau stated that 'cultural pluralism is the very essence of Canadian identity'. A policy of multiculturalism would seek to secure every ethnic group 'the right to preserve and develop its own culture and values within the Canadian context'.[18] Across the border in the United States, cultural pluralism would also become more prominent (although the US has never adopted an official multiculturalism). In both countries there was in the 1970s a departure from the assimilationist model of immigrant settlement. The cultural differences of foreign arrivals would now be tolerated – even encouraged. Governments moved to root out racial discrimination and reform educational curricula, and in many cases provided public funding of ethnic associations and festivals.

All this didn't emerge out of nowhere. There was political lobbying and pressure from immigrant groups in Australia, Canada and the US.[19] Perhaps more decisively, demands for multicultural recognition were part of a broader rights revolution. Notions of racial or ethnic hierarchy, once widely accepted by Western nations, were thoroughly discredited in the immediate aftermath of the Second World War, as the full extent of Nazi Germany's program of racial purification and extermination was exposed. The Universal Declaration of Human Rights in 1948, the rapid process of decolonisation in Africa and Asia, and the civil rights struggle to eliminate racial segregation in the US would cumulatively add momentum to multiculturalism. There was a new consciousness about rights and race, ethnicity and equality. As with the different phases of the postwar 'human rights revolution', multiculturalism rejected ethnic and racial hierarchies. The only thing different was that it sought to 'apply this commitment more effectively to the actual range of exclusions, stigmatisations, and inequalities that exist in Western democracies' – as opposed to those that existed outside them.[20]

In its original phase, a multicultural approach to immigrant settlement was a question of social justice. Could there really be equality of opportunity, Grassby asked, if the cultural identities and heritage of citizens from immigrant backgrounds is 'denied the dignity of self-expression and self-determination'? There would be grave consequences to ignoring diversity, whether that involved 'explosive pressures' or 'naked repression'.[21] From the outset, we can see that equity and participation were as much concerns for the likes of Grassby and Whitlam – and Trudeau – as any cultural pluralism. Multiculturalism was a response to the social and economic disadvantages immigrants were experiencing, especially in work, education and health. The landmark Henderson Poverty Inquiry conducted in the early 1970s, for example, revealed that certain immigrant groups were suffering from exceptionally high rates of poverty.[22] It was no longer good enough, as Whitlam observed in one speech, to 'assume that mere permission to settle among us is a boon of such transcendental quality that simple gratitude and silent compliance are the sole duties of those upon whom this benefit is conferred'. In all spheres of society, 'we should no longer expect migrants to settle for the second rate, particularly when so much of what passes for our best is itself second rate by the standards of the countries with which we compare ourselves'.[23]

Multiculturalism would mean nothing if it didn't ultimately strengthen the ability of citizens to become full participants in society.

The emphasis on social justice has led some scholars to suggest that the Whitlam government never embraced multiculturalism with enthusiasm.[24] This diagnosis doesn't seem correct. There was in the early 1970s a definitive shift from assimilationist Anglo-conformity towards a multicultural society. The White Australia policy, much of whose architecture had been slowly dismantled by Liberal governments during the 1960s, was finally being put to rest. 'It is dead', Whitlam would say in 1974, echoing earlier remarks from Grassby in 1973: 'Give me a shovel and I will bury it'.[25] The remnants of a racially discriminatory immigration program were removed. Assisted passage, once offered only to Europeans, was offered to non-Europeans as well. Among other things, no immigration official would now have the discretionary right to determine whether an arrival was sufficiently 'European' to be allowed in. They would be gatekeepers to a White Australia no longer.

There were also important welfare and legal reforms entrenching the multicultural ideal. The Australian Assistance Plan was introduced, indirectly providing a system of welfare services for immigrants. Regional Councils of Social Development, which were responsible for the Plan, would be 'the catalyst for the first significant attempt on the part of ethnic groups to combine, in order to represent common ethnic interests in public affairs'.[26] Most of the Councils included a committee devoted to issues concerning immigrants – these would become the forerunners of the state ethnic communities councils that exist today as peak representative bodies.

On the legal front, being a British subject resident in Australia no longer entitled one to enjoy special privileges such as the easier attainment of citizenship and visas. The deportation of naturalised Australians to their native country under the *Crimes Act* became a thing of the past. Perhaps the most important development was the passage of the *Racial Discrimination Act* of 1975. Any 'discrimination, exclusion, restriction or preference based on race, colour, descent or national or ethnic origin' was, under the Act, outlawed. The legislation also established a Community Relations Council, led by a Commissioner, invested with powers to investigate alleged cases of racial discrimination. (Al Grassby would become the inaugural Commissioner, after losing his seat in parliament in 1974.) According to Whitlam in 1975, 'The new Act writes it firmly into our laws that Australia is in reality a multicultural nation, in which the linguistic and cultural heritage of the Aboriginal people and of peoples from all parts of the world can find an honoured place.'[27]

In abolishing White Australia, recognising the marginalised status of immigrant minorities and finally creating a legal apparatus of anti-discrimination, the Whitlam government laid the foundations of official Australian multiculturalism. As historian Gwenda Tavan observes, these reforms embodied 'the unequivocal rejection of a policy and doctrine that had enjoyed almost hegemonic status in Australian public life'. By 'endowing the issue of non-racial-discrimination in public policy with a strong moral authority', the Whitlam government erected a political barrier against the overt politicisation of racial issues by future governments and political parties – though in time this barrier would be placed under pressure. Moreover, it presented Australians with a reconfigured national identity, replacing overtly racial and racist dimensions with 'tolerance of a measure of cultural and racial pluralism'.[28]

From cultural pluralism to citizenship

It wasn't until the late 1970s that Australia's credentials as a fledgling multicultural society would meet its first serious test. The challenge took the form of Indochinese refugees, primarily from Vietnam, who would arrive in Australia in the aftermath of the protracted Indochinese conflict. It was the decision of then Liberal Prime Minister Malcolm Fraser to accept an influx of refugees. This wasn't without its political risks. The steady increase in the arrival of Vietnamese 'boat people' revived old anxieties about Asian hordes 'invading' Australia. Though things began innocuously enough in 1976, with a single vessel carrying five people slipping into Darwin harbour, very quickly Vietnamese boat arrivals became a daily occurrence. By the middle of 1978 more than 1000 boat people had arrived.

Much as Whitlam did before him, Fraser would initially resist increasing the Australian intake of refugees.[29] But by 1979 the scale of the crisis was evident. Refugee camps throughout South-East Asia were overflowing. Boats were arriving with no sign their numbers would ease. The Fraser government received advice from within the Department of Immigration and Ethnic Affairs that the arrival of refugees had 'all the ingredients for one of the most controversial and divisive issues in Australia's history'. The government was warned about the likelihood of '[a] hostile public reaction, stimulated by traditional fears of the "yellow peril" and by concern about present high levels of unemployment'.[30] Nevertheless, the Fraser government decided to accept more refugees. By 1983, it had resettled some 70 000 Indochinese refugees in Australia. Per head of population, Australia took in the largest number of Indochinese refugees of any country in the world.

Refugees from the Indochinese conflict weren't the only source of increased Asian immigration during the Fraser years. The late 1970s saw an increase in overall immigration levels. In Whitlam's final year in office, the immigration intake stood at just over 50 000. By the 1980s, entry levels would exceed 100 000 a year, with immigrants from Asia accounting for close to 30 per cent of the total intake. The expansion of the family reunion program in 1978 opened the way for further immigrants from Asia to arrive. In his memoirs, Fraser reflected that his boost to immigration and intake of refugees 'gave substance to the ending of the White Australia policy'.[31] During Fraser's prime ministership, Australia had crossed the multicultural threshold, and not only in the abstract. What was once a white Australia had opened its doors not only to southern Europeans with olive skin but now also Asians with yellow.

There can be no doubting Fraser's role in consolidating cultural pluralism. He was a strong advocate for this new reality. 'In multiculturalism', he said in one speech, Australians had found 'a basis which offers at once both an understanding of the present and vision of the future built upon that understanding'.[32] Multiculturalism was here to stay. And it was given a new comprehensive statement in the *Review of Post-Arrival Programs and Services to Migrants* of 1978, commissioned by Fraser and regarded by him as a personal project. The Galbally Report, as it became known, was to define government policies on immigrant settlement and integration for much of the next decade. According to the report, multiculturalism was a matter of accepting a diversity of cultural identities, within the limits of an Australian national community:

We are convinced that migrants have the right to maintain their cultural and racial identity and that it is clearly in the best interests of our nation that they should be encouraged and assisted to do so if they wish. Provided that ethnic identity is not stressed at the expense of society at large, but is interwoven into the fabric of our nationhood by the process of multicultural interaction, then the community as a whole will benefit substantially and its democratic nature will be reinforced. The knowledge that people are identified with their cultural background and ethnic group enables them to take their place in their new society with confidence if their ethnicity has been accepted by the community.[33]

The Galbally Report outlined the institutions of a 'cultural pluralist' model of multiculturalism, which emphasised the tolerance of cultural differences. In tabling the report to parliament himself, Fraser argued in favour of 'the retention of the cultural heritage of different ethnic groups and promotion of intercultural understanding'.[34] If a doctrine of assimilation had meant that governments should be perfectly indifferent to people's cultural identities, one of multiculturalism meant that there should be some degree of differential treatment. Equal rights mightn't be served by identical treatment. In a culturally diverse society, equality might require some provision of public services tailored specifically for minorities.

This would inform the recommendations of the Galbally Report on settlement programs, which encompassed the provision of English language courses and improvements to immigrants' access to the legal, health and welfare systems. On these matters, the Fraser government adopted a devolved approach. Ethnic communities rather than government departments would be given most direct control over settlement services such as English-language classes – namely, through government-funded migrant resource centres and a community-based welfare system of grant-in-aid social workers.

But it was another recommendation of Galbally's which would have perhaps the widest-ranging effect on multiculturalism yet. The creation of the Special Broadcasting Service (SBS) as a multicultural television station, independent and separate from the Australian Broadcasting Corporation (ABC), would ensure a permanent 'ethnic' presence on the television airwaves. While SBS's initial aim was primarily to help new arrivals acquaint themselves with life in Australia, it would evolve over subsequent decades to promote understanding of diversity among the general population.

By the time Fraser lost power in 1983, a significant shift in multicultural policy was about to occur. Although bipartisanship on questions of cultural diversity and immigration was by now established, the early years of the Hawke government indicated the next, third stage in official multiculturalism. In contrast to Fraser's cultural pluralist approach, Hawke argued in 1984 that multiculturalism was 'an approach to policy formulation and resource allocation which seeks to provide for equality and access and opportunity'.[35] Renewed attention was placed on using multicultural policy to address the socioeconomic needs of immigrants. There was a more powerful recognition that some newly arrived Australians were disadvantaged because of their culture and ethnicity, because of discrimination and prejudice. It wasn't enough to support cultural maintenance without also addressing more structural matters.

There remained, of course, a good deal of continuity between the Fraser and Hawke years. Australia continued to grow increasingly diverse in its ethnic and cultural complexion, as a result of a sustained intake of immigrants. After a brief decline in immigration following the recession of 1982–83, the net intake of immigrants would climb to over 170 000 in 1987–88. By that year, 39 per cent of Australia's immigrants would come from Asia, compared to 21 per cent from the UK and Ireland. But in the second half of the 1980s, multiculturalism as policy took on a more distinctive accent of social justice. The Jupp Review of Migrant and Multicultural Programs and Services in 1986 highlighted 'the link between multiculturalism and the economic and social rights of people from a non-English-speaking background'.[36] In calling for 'the equitable participation of overseas-born residents in Australian society', the Jupp w added force to the Hawke government's 'access and equity' strategy, outlined in 1985. This social justice focus diverged from the Galbally model of cultural pluralism, which was primarily concerned with ethnic-specific government services. The emphasis now would be on achieving a better balance between 'mainstream' and 'ethnic-specific' policies and programs. While some of the latter would be retained, government policy after the Jupp Review would prioritise the reform of mainstream service delivery.

Momentum for multiculturalism was stalled by one thing: the 1986 federal budget saw a series of savage funding cuts to multicultural programs, as Hawke and then Treasurer Paul Keating sought to impose fiscal discipline in the face of a current account deficit. But this would ultimately prove a mere hiccup. By the end of the decade, multiculturalism emerged resurgent and more muscular than ever before. The Office of Multicultural Affairs (OMA) was established as a branch within the Department of Prime Minister and Cabinet, ensuring that multicultural issues were placed at the heart of government policy formation. Charged with devising an updated, comprehensive multicultural philosophy, OMA produced in 1989 the *National Agenda for a Multicultural Australia*. A document widely regarded as the most impressive statement yet of multiculturalism as a prescription, the *National Agenda* reformulated the social justice concerns that had featured so prominently during the 1970s.[37] It did this in two ways. First, it reiterated the necessity of an access and equity strategy in changing 'the management culture of our public administration' so as to 'make Commonwealth departments [respond] equitably – and efficiently – to a culturally diverse clientele'. Second, it included social justice explicitly in its definition of multiculturalism. It was 'the right of all Australians to equality of treatment and opportunity', regardless of their 'race, ethnicity, culture, religion, language, gender or place of birth'. Social justice would be listed as one of the three dimensions of multiculturalism as a policy, alongside cultural identity and economic efficiency.[38]

What held this together was a new understanding of *citizenship*. Multiculturalism, the *National Agenda* emphasised, wasn't a policy whose relevance was confined to ethnic minorities and immigrants – it was a policy for all Australians. Such a view was possible because tolerance and respect for cultural diversity were no longer viewed as demands of cultural pluralism. Rather, as the language of access and equity suggested, they were regarded more fundamentally as demands of civic equality. Multiculturalism would defend 'the right of all Australians ... to express their individual cultural heritage, including their language and religion'. Such freedom came with full membership of the Australian political community, and was accompanied by responsibilities. Any cultural right to express one's identity and beliefs involved a responsibility to offer 'an overriding and unifying commitment to Australia', and to its civic culture:

> multicultural policies require all Australians to
> accept the basic structures and principles of
> Australian society – the Constitution and the
> rule of law, tolerance and equality, parliamentary
> democracy, freedom of speech and religion, English
> as the national language and equality of the sexes
> . . .[39]

Multiculturalism may have repudiated the older model of homogeneous nationhood reflected in the stance of cultural assimilation, but this didn't mean that it repudiated nationhood altogether.

By the start of the 1990s, therefore, Australian multiculturalism had progressed from its early phase as a rupture from assimilation, and from its later incarnation as cultural pluralism. It had developed into a nation-building policy based on an ideal of citizenship. Diversity wasn't meant to undermine or supersede the Australian nation. This runs counter to the frequently made assumption that multiculturalism can only take root in a 'post-national' state and society. 'In reality', as political philosopher Will Kymlicka observes, the sort of multiculturalism that has emerged within the West has transformed nation-building, not replaced it'.[40] So it was in Australia, and emphatically so.

Multiculturalism under attack, and its recovery

Not all Australians supported the development of multiculturalism during the 1970s and 80s. Throughout the period, there were always opponents of multicultural policy, if not also of a multicultural society. Very few organised groups would express their opposition through overt appeals to racist ideals of a white Australia (one notable exception being Jack van Tongeren's far-right Australian Nationalist Movement, which was responsible for a series of firebombings targeting Chinese restaurants in Perth during the 1980s). Only occasionally did crude bigotry present itself in public – as it did in 1987, when Sydney talkback radio presenter Ron Casey, responding to a caller's complaint about her husband's unemployment, suggested that her husband have his eyes surgically altered to look 'slopey, slopey, one-uppy, one-downy', so as to look Chinese and gain special treatment at government social security offices.[41] Yet, with multiculturalism gathering new momentum as official policy, considerable hostility towards cultural diversity remained. The opposition to multiculturalism would be tied increasingly to anxieties about the impact of Asian immigration, as two key episodes would highlight.

The first began innocuously enough. It was St Patrick's Day, 1984. In an old cinema theatre in Warrnambool, western Victoria, delegates to a Rotary Club conference gathered to hear prominent historian Geoffrey Blainey. The speech he delivered would ordinarily have gone unnoticed – were it not for his criticism of the pace of Asian immigration. 'Rarely in the history of the modern world', Blainey argued, 'has a nation given such preference to a tiny ethnic minority of its population as the Australian government has done in the past few years'. Asians were now the 'favoured majority' in Australia's immigration intake. According to Blainey – who would elaborate his position in the prolonged national debate sparked by his Warrnambool speech – Asian immigration and multiculturalism were out of touch with the views of 'everyday Australians'. This was, in his view, particularly true of those 'old Australians who live in the front-line suburbs' where Asian immigrants were most likely to settle. These 'old Australians' were under siege in suburbs such as Sydney's Cabramatta or Melbourne's Springvale. There, he argued, the Australian way of life was being radically transformed – whether it was the pavements spotted with phlegm, the smell of exotic meat, or the noodles being dried out in backyards.[42] Blainey believed that multiculturalism had cut 'the crimson thread of kinship', a reference to Henry Parkes's famous invocation of British race patriotism. 'The cult of the immigrant, the emphasis on separateness for ethnic groups, the wooing of Asian and the shunning of Britain', he concluded, 'are part of this thread-cutting'.[43] In his view, Asian immigrants were conducting a quiet colonisation of the country.

Blainey's intervention was met with a blizzard of criticism, including from his own colleagues in the Department of History at the University of Melbourne (24 of whom would sign a public letter in *The Age*, repudiating his views). Yet its impact was profound: the Blainey critique was widely publicised and triggered an ugly debate. As the first prominent Australian to express such forthright opposition, Blainey mounted an important challenge to the multicultural consensus in warning of Australia descending into a 'nation of tribes'. His impact – as did his rhetoric – arguably resembled that of the British Conservative politician Enoch Powell. In his infamous 'Rivers of Blood' speech in 1968, Powell declared that Britain, by virtue of immigration, had become a 'nation busily engaged in heaping up its own funeral pyre', with indigenous white Britons destined to become 'strangers in their own country'. With his allusion to the ancient poet Virgil, Powell forecast grave racial conflict: 'As I look ahead, I am filled with foreboding; like the Roman, I seem to see "the River Tiber foaming with much blood".'[44] Albeit with less colour than Powell, Blainey had clearly marked out the battlelines.

The second key attack on multiculturalism came in 1988 from then federal opposition leader John Howard. It more or less repeated Blainey's line of argument. That is, multiculturalism failed to reflect the sentiments of Australia's suburban heartland, failed to ensure social cohesion, and failed to do justice to Australia's British heritage. Howard's opposition emerged in a year of much heated debate. A government-appointed inquiry into immigration policy, led by Australia's first ambassador to China, Stephen FitzGerald, reported a troubling disjunction between the official definition of multiculturalism and how it was popularly understood. The FitzGerald Report, as the inquiry's final document came to be known, warned there was a negative perception of multiculturalism as a policy that was 'sectional and divisive', representing something for immigrants and ethnic communities only. Such sentiments couldn't be dismissed as 'simply the voice of extremism, or racism', as they were 'undermining public support for immigration'.[45] Emboldened by the Fitzgerald Report's concerns about social cohesion and Australian identity, Howard called for a 'full and open debate on the direction of Australia's immigration policy'.[46] He did his part by raising questions about whether the levels of Asian immigration to Australia could be absorbed by the Australian population. 'There are some in the community who are concerned that the pace of change has been too great,' Howard said. To raise the point was 'not to be racist but to be realistic'. Howard called for the abolition of multiculturalism as a policy, arguing that it amounted to social fragmentation and to 'some kind of apology for being Australian'. In its place, Howard proposed a 'One Australia' approach that would celebrate 'an authentic Australian culture'.

Howard's attack marked the first significant departure from the political bipartisanship that had existed on immigration since the end of the Second World War – and on multiculturalism since its inception in the 1970s. It didn't end well for Howard. His dual assault on Asian immigration and multiculturalism was widely regarded as a dangerous form of race politics. The editorial prognosis of the *Australian Financial Review* in August 1988, which noted that 'once uncorked the racial argument rampages at will, and has a cannibalistic capacity to devour its progenitors', turned out to be correct.[47] The Hawke government's response of a parliamentary motion affirming Australia's commitment to a non-discriminatory immigration policy saw senior Liberals, including one Philip Ruddock (a future Immigration Minister and Attorney-General in the Howard government), cross the floor to vote with Labor. A number of prominent Liberals outside the federal parliament, including Malcolm Fraser and then New South Wales premier Nick Greiner, also rebuked Howard. The whole episode was pivotal in setting the scene for Howard's removal as federal Liberal leader in 1989.

It was also instrumental in putting greater pressure on the Hawke government at the time to clarify the meaning of multiculturalism. The implementation of the *National Agenda*, with its emphasis on citizenship and the expression of cultural diversity within the limits of an Australian national identity, clearly reflected the impact of the attacks on multiculturalism and Asian immigration. By the end of the 1980s, it was increasingly recognised that the public acceptance of cultural diversity couldn't be taken for granted. If the reality of cultural diversity was to be supported by a policy of multiculturalism, there had to be a more compelling way of communicating its necessity. The value of multiculturalism couldn't be confined to just immigrants and 'ethnics', but had to extend to all Australians.

This imperative perhaps explains why multiculturalism during the Keating years took on a more economistic slant. The idea of 'productive diversity' set much of the tone. Developed by the OMA, this approach emphasised the economic benefits of recognising cultural diversity. At one level, productive diversity reflected a response to globalisation and Australian integration with Asia. As a result of the landmark 1989 White Paper on Asia written by economist Ross Garnaut, *Australia and the North-East Asian Ascendancy*, it became a more urgent priority to link Australia more closely with the economies of Asia.[48] Faced with a mounting current account deficit, the Australian economy could only in the long run trade its way out. Asia would provide the export markets, foreign investment and skilled immigrants required for the task.

The thrust of the productive diversity argument was unambiguous. As expressed in the subtitle of an OMA discussion paper, it was about 'profiting from Australia's multicultural advantage'.[49] Multiculturalism became a tool for managing the transition to a globalised Australian economy, three-quarters of whose trade was conducted with non-English speaking countries, principally in Asia. In order to improve economic performance, 'more managers will need to modify Australia's traditional approach to export negotiations and develop their capacity to deal across cultural barriers in the much more pro-active style of traders in Asia'.[50] Whether it lay in linguistic skills, cultural knowledge or commercial networks, a multicultural workforce was a source of wealth whose potential wasn't fully tapped. In other words, multiculturalism had a practical pay-off. Much like those European immigrants who came to work on the Snowy Mountains Scheme, the Asian immigrants of the 1980s, 1990s and beyond would provide the basis for national economic prosperity. It was the job of multiculturalism as policy to make it happen.

This didn't mean there was a break from the Hawke era, though some believe that Keating was never as effusive as Hawke about multicultural policy. In his opening address to an international conference on cultural diversity in 1995, Keating stressed the relationship between multiculturalism and citizenship. As he explained, 'That is the essential balance in the multicultural equation: the promotion of individual and collective rights and expression, on the one hand; and on the other, the promotion of common national interests and values.'[51] Amid the gathering pace of debates about national identity, this civic dimension of multiculturalism enjoyed continued emphasis. Where its critics saw it as a source of social division, supporters of multicultural citizenship saw it as filling the void left by discredited racialised notions of Australian identity. Australian citizenship, defined by adherence to parliamentary democracy, free speech and tolerance, was ultimately the bond that everyone shared. This predominantly civic definition of national identity left room for Australians of all ethnic backgrounds to feel that they were part of the nation.

Productive diversity didn't come to define official multiculturalism entirely, even if cultural and economic questions were regularly fused into one. During the Keating years multiculturalism became part of a broader project of national reinvention, or what Keating described as the 'big picture'. The 1980s and 1990s were a period of modernising the Australian economy: the dollar was floated, the banking sector deregulated; tariff walls were lifted. Keating believed this should be extended to what he called the reform of our outlook. In his view, 'the economic imperative and the cultural one can't be separated – they have the same conclusion'. The destination was that of a new, confident, independent Australia – a nation 'sure of who we are and what we stand for'.[52]

For Keating, all vestiges of what he called the 'old Australia' were gone. The familiar certainties of the British Empire, White Australia and a protected economy could never be restored. The only path available was for the nation to remake itself. As journalist Paul Kelly explains, the various elements of Keating's vision were in 'wonderful harmony'.[53] Australia needed to make the transition from a constitutional monarchy to a republic, achieve reconciliation with its Indigenous population, and become fully integrated into Asia. And it would be doing all these things as an emphatically multicultural nation. Keating's embrace of multiculturalism was a nationalistic and patriotic one. It formed part of his 'radical nationalist' understanding of nationhood, one which believed Australian identity had to be liberated from its derivative attachment to Britain. Embracing multiculturalism wasn't so much about responding to cultural diversity – it was a condition for realising a national destiny.

The legacy of Hanson and Howard

Keating's project of national reinvention didn't survive the 1996 election, in which the Coalition triumphed under the resurrected leadership of John Howard. Australia would be taking a more conservative course under the Howard government. As Howard's comments in 1988 demonstrated, he was no friend of multiculturalism, even if in 1995 he tried to make amends by acknowledging the offence he had caused to many Australians of Asian descent. In its first year his government moved swiftly to abolish the Office of Multicultural Affairs and the Bureau of Immigration, Multiculturalism and Population

Research, two key agencies in the policy architecture of multiculturalism (the functions of these agencies were transferred to the Department of Immigration).

As it turned out, the biggest challenge to multiculturalism would come from a different source. When the newly elected member for the Queensland seat of Oxley rose in the House of Representatives on 10 September 1996, to a largely empty chamber, few would have anticipated the speaker would spark such a national controversy. Delivering her maiden speech, Pauline Hanson railed against the 'reverse racism' perpetrated by politically correct 'fat cats', 'do-gooders' and 'bureaucrats' against 'mainstream Australians'. In addition to Aboriginals, whom she claimed were enjoying special privileges over and above all other Australians, Hanson had in her sights those members of what she called the 'multicultural industries':

Immigration and multiculturalism are issues that this government is trying to address, but for far too long ordinary Australians have been kept out of any debate by the major parties. I and most Australians want our immigration policy radically reviewed and that of multiculturalism abolished. I believe we are in danger of being swamped by Asians. Between 1984 and 1995, 40 per cent of all migrants coming into this country were of Asian origin. They have their own culture and religion, form ghettos and do not assimilate. Of course, I will be called racist, but if I can invite whom I want into my home, then I should have the right to have a say in who comes into my country. A truly multicultural country can never be strong or united. The world is full of failed and tragic examples, ranging from Ireland to Bosnia to Africa and, closer to home, Papua New Guinea. America and Great Britain are currently paying the price.[54]

Within weeks of Hanson's speech, which attracted extensive media coverage at home and abroad, a network of supporters had emerged. By April 1997, Pauline Hanson's One Nation party had come into being. At the party's launch, Hanson posed for pictures draped in the Australian flag and promoted a book that was ostensibly her manifesto, *Pauline Hanson: The Truth*. Partly written by members of the Pauline Hanson Support Movement, the forerunners of One Nation, the book forecasted that Australia in 2050 would a 1.8-billion-strong republic integrated into the 'United States of Asia', and ruled by President Poona Li Hung, a part-cyborg Malaysian lesbian of Chinese and Indian descent.[55] In this bizarre future, white Australians are a persecuted minority, a relic of a society and civilisation that had been, in no uncertain terms, swamped by Asia.

While it may have been dystopian fantasy, the scenario of *Pauline Hanson: The Truth* nonetheless revealed the 'deep-seated fears of cultural decline and loss' felt by Hanson's supporters.[56] For Hanson and her followers, successive national governments had betrayed ordinary Australians. Elite political correctness was corroding the wholesome values of the Australian people.

In one sense, Hansonism reflected the uneven impact that economic rationalism had on Australian society. Its rise was a symptom of 'a burgeoning gulf between a largely urban and cosmopolitan Australia and the hinterland where the rewards of deregulatory reforms have been scarce'.[57] Yet it was the cultural language of Hansonism which lent the movement its political potency. Hanson's call for restricting Asian immigration and for returning to assimilation – she drew upon the example of Arthur Calwell in her maiden speech – appealed to an unvarnished nostalgia for an Australia of old. At the same time, Hansonism deployed an identity politics based on grievance and resentment. It sought to correct a perceived 'disrespect' or 'misrecognition' of a traditional Anglo-Celtic Australian identity by political elites.[58] Especially at fault were the policy of multiculturalism and the policy of Aboriginal reconciliation, both of which offered preferential treatment to minorities at the expense of white Australians. Hansonism sought to reinstate the spirit of 'one nation' against the supposedly destructive influences of diversity.

This rhetoric replicated the arguments for a White Australia. In the case of the latter, restrictions on non-

European immigrants were regarded as necessary safeguards for social stability and an expression of national self-determination. Similarly, One Nation framed its policies as founded on a principle of sovereignty. One early policy document declared that 'Australians, like other peoples of the world, have the right to maintain their unique identity and culture' and that 'it is never immoral to want to retain one's own independence and identity'.[59] But it would be a mistake to dismiss Hansonism as an explosion of simplistic, one-dimensional racism, as many believed.

This isn't to deny that Hanson's stance on immigration, multiculturalism and Indigenous affairs provoked racist sentiments among some of its supporters. Her language was inflammatory; her logic crude. As much as Hansonism depicted 'elites' as the enemies of ordinary Australians, it also scapegoated Asian immigrants and Aboriginals, and made them targets of abuse. While Hanson's supporters believed that an Anglo-Celtic Australian identity was being disrespected, they failed to notice that they might also have been guilty of the same crime toward some of their fellow citizens.

Ultimately, Hansonism was a movement of nationalist populism. The philosopher and historian of ideas Isaiah Berlin once famously wrote about the 'bent twig' of nationalism: like a twig that springs back and whips the face of the person who has touched it, nationalism was at root a collective response to a perceived slight or provocation. It is typically 'a response to a patronising or disparaging attitude towards the traditional values of a society, the result of wounded pride and a sense of humiliation in its most socially conscious members, which in due course produce anger and self-assertion'.[60] The Hansonist movement was nothing if not a very bent twig of Australian nationalism.

Few understood this better than Howard, himself no stranger to controversy arising from immigration and multiculturalism. His immediate response to Hanson's maiden speech was to defend her right to express her views. To be fair, it wasn't only the Liberal–National coalition that adopted a wait-and-see approach at first: Labor was also slow off the mark in condemning Hanson, although it consistently placed One Nation last in its how to vote cards, unlike the Coalition. The most prominent critics of Hanson in 1996 and 1997 were community groups in civil society, many of which coalesced as the Anti-Racist Campaign. But it was Howard who was best placed to capitalise on the nationalist populism unleashed in 1996. When the tide of Hansonism receded, which it quickly did, Howard was there to claim Hanson's supporters.

Howard's worldview had an evident, natural affinity with Hanson's. The very language of 'One Nation' wasn't far off from 'One Australia', the name of the policy Howard adopted when he launched his own attack on multiculturalism in 1988. In the 1996 election campaign,

Howard ran on the slogan of 'For All of Us' – the idea being that the Liberal Party would heal the alleged division caused by Keating's agenda of national reinvention. Howard's ideological conservatism was defined by the idea of the 'mainstream'. This stood in opposition to a supposedly elite, pro-Labor, left-wing Establishment, which was entrenched in the universities, the media (particularly the ABC), welfare organisations and in the arts. The mainstream 'became a code, an impulse that connected Howard to the people'.[61] It would become the backbone of Howard's own brand of nationalism, which in turn was increasingly shaping the 'culture wars' during his prime ministership.

Whichever way you look at it, multiculturalism occupied a deeply ambivalent place in Howard's mainstream Australia. Howard personally avoided using the word for much of the period that he was Prime Minister. It wasn't until 2005 that Howard would come, grudgingly, to accept that 'multiculturalism means a lot of things, different things to different people, but in its lowest common denominator it means that people believe in diversity and are therefore tolerant of racial and ethnic difference'.[62]

Almost curiously, given Howard's well-documented aversion to multiculturalism, his government never actively dismantled multicultural policy in one sense. (Some attribute this to the influence of his long-serving chief of staff, now Senator for New South Wales, Arthur

Sinodinos.) The citizenship model of multiculturalism survived almost the full duration of the Howard government's four terms. It would even be given a more emphatically nation-building focus. A new National Multicultural Advisory Council was appointed in 1997 and charged with the task of 'ensuring that cultural diversity is a unifying force of Australia'. The Council's recommendations – which included retaining the term 'multiculturalism', but adding the prefix 'Australian' – would be supported in the government's resulting 1999 policy document, *A New Agenda for Multicultural Australia*. 'Australian multiculturalism' was embraced as a term which both celebrated cultural diversity and recognised 'civic duty'.[63] This was updated in the 2003 policy document, *Multicultural Australia: United in Diversity*.[64]

There was, however, one glitch: at the expiration of the *Multicultural Australia: United in Diversity* policy at the end of 2006, the Howard government never issued a succeeding policy document.[65] While this meant that, in effect, the policy was allowed to die out, it didn't mean the death of multiculturalism at large. It perhaps simply meant that the centre of gravity in policy terms shifted from the Commonwealth level to the States (which have well-established anti-discrimination and equal opportunity legislation, and operate their various multicultural, community and ethnic affairs commissions).[66]

But the tension between multiculturalism and the conservatism of the Howard years was evident. On the one hand, up until 2006 multiculturalism remained in place as a policy and immigration levels increased substantially – with a growing proportion coming from Asia. On the other hand, the tone of the political debate during the Howard years grew increasingly hostile towards multiculturalism. The assertion of 'mainstream' values aimed to close down debate about national identity. According to Howard, 'I think we've come back from being too obsessed with diversity to a point where we are very proud and conscious of those ongoing, distinctive, defining characteristics of being an Australian which we tend to identify with what I might call the old Australia'.[67] Howard railed against 'self-appointed cultural dieticians who tell us that in some way they know better what an Australian ought to be than all of us who know what an Australian has always been and always will be'.[68] This was a Prime Minister who triumphantly declared the debate about what it meant to be Australian over – as though such debates could ever be resolved like a high school debate. The nation, in his eyes, was now far too 'relaxed and comfortable' to bother with 'elite' concerns such as multiculturalism.

The impact of the Howard government went beyond the symbolic terrain of the culture wars. Most notably, there was its adoption of a hardline position on asylum seekers. Encapsulated by the *Tampa* incident of 2001, in which Afghan refugees rescued at sea by a Norwegian cargo ship were prevented from landing on Australian territory, and the introduction of a 'Pacific solution' to the arrival of asylum seekers by boat, this approach would inject a new toxin into the body politic. The old bipartisan approach to keeping race out of Australian politics, successively challenged by Blainey in 1984, Howard in 1988 and Hanson in 1996, crumbled during Howard's period as Prime Minister. The debate on asylum seekers, in which 'boat people' were frequently depicted as queue-jumpers motivated by economic ambition, was increasingly used for the public airing of racism and anxiety about cultural difference.

Meanwhile, concerns about social cohesion and Muslims – heightened by the September 11 attacks of 2001, the Bali bombing of 2002 and the London bombings of 2005 – led to an increasingly muscular imposition of 'Australian values'. This was most evident in the introduction in 2007 of a citizenship test for immigrants who wished to naturalise. Although the idea of a citizenship test itself is by no means objectionable, what was striking was the manner in which the test became a vehicle for the promotion of a certain cultural nationalism.[69] It wasn't enough, for instance, that prospective citizens were tested about civic values and democracy: they would also have to answer questions about cricketer Donald Bradman and effectively prove that they weren't 'un-Australian'. The increasingly tense social environment – claims of a relaxed and comfortable Australia notwithstanding – was highlighted in the 2005

Cronulla riot. In what was arguably an unprecedented loss of domestic civil order, a 5000-strong mob took to the streets in the Sydney beachside suburb, searching for 'Lebs' and anyone of Middle Eastern appearance to attack. Howard's response was to reaffirm that 'there is no underlying racism in Australian society'.[70]

That Howard could offer such a response reflected the confident grip he had on the Australian psyche. There had been a profound reorientation of Australian political culture since 1996. The terms of debate had changed. Political scientist Judith Brett makes the convincing case that Howard married an ideological tradition of Australian liberalism with the repertoire of radical nationalism. As represented by 'the Australian Legend',[71] such nationalism celebrated the distinctive qualities of an Australian character defined by egalitarianism, mateship and scepticism of authority. Once 'owned' by Labor, the Legend had been gradually abandoned as the party moved increasingly towards its progressive middle-class supporters and away from its traditional working-class base. Cultural nationalism didn't seem to fit with a new multicultural Australia: thus, while Keating's brand of radical nationalism represented something of an effort at a reconciliation of old and new Australia, his politics were more often than not understood as something rather more cosmopolitan. In the shadow of Keating's loss in 1996, and Labor's struggle to articulate a cultural narrative, it was left to Howard to claim the Legend for his purposes.[72]

It was only in 2007 that Howard belatedly gave this peculiar interpretation of Australian liberal conservatism a name. It was 'aspirational nationalism', a model that blended the economic and social components of Howard's political philosophy. If Keating's mission of remaking Australia had involved an ideological 'package' (a multicultural republic, engagement with Asia, Aboriginal reconciliation and economic modernisation), so did Howard's reinstatement of an old Australia.[73] The nationalist part of the equation was unambiguous: in place of Keating's supposed cosmopolitanism there was the rediscovery of Gallipoli and the Anzac legend, an unapologetic celebration of an Australian national character and way of life. As for aspiration, this was the economic component of Howard's ideological package, founded on traditional Liberal sympathies to enterprise, small business and families: free market reforms such as privatisation and industrial relations liberalisation, and welfare support through measures such as family tax benefits.

Armed with this aspirational nationalism, Howard's politics were a creative appropriation of Hanson's populism. The marginalised mob of Hanson had been transformed into a mainstream mob. If Hansonism was the product of the anxieties that existed in a traditional Australian hinterland, Howard's aspirational nationalism was built on the anxieties of those in the suburbs. But in both cases, their constituencies perceived themselves to have been cut adrift from an urban, progressive Australia that saw in cultural diversity and multiculturalism only opportunities and never any threats.

The political culture of today's Australia still bears the mark of this development. The arrival of the Rudd government in 2007 didn't change things dramatically. It wasn't until 2008 that the Rudd government moved to fill the policy vacuum left by its predecessor by creating the Australian Multicultural Advisory Council. The terms of any policy didn't emerge until late 2010 with the adoption of the *People of Australia* document and the establishment of an Australian Multicultural Council (on which I serve as an appointed member). There has since been, as I've noted, the appointment of a Minister for Multicultural Affairs, Senator Kate Lundy. But it remains to be seen whether a substantial renewal of Australian multiculturalism as national policy will take place, and if so, how.

While the Gillard government has been moderately enthusiastic, this attitude doesn't seem to be shared by the Coalition. In a speech in April 2012, opposition leader Tony Abbott could only offer a lukewarm reference to multiculturalism as 'officialese for Australians' traditional acceptance of newcomers' attachment to old ways while they get used to new ones'.[74] The Shadow Minister for Immigration and Citizenship, Scott Morrison, has publicly noted that 'I am always reluctant to use the term multiculturalism'.[75] In 2011, Morrison was even reported to have urged his shadow cabinet colleagues to exploit public concerns about 'Muslim immigration' and to ramp up its questioning of 'multiculturalism'.[76] Meanwhile, in 2012, Morrison's colleague Teresa Gambaro, the Shadow Parliamentary Secretary for Citizenship and Settlement, caused extensive public controversy by suggesting that immigrants should be taught to wear deodorant – a move many regarded as a maladroit act of dog-whistling.[77] These are hardly reassuring signs that Australia has moved on from the populist legacies of Hanson and Howard.

2

The Australian model

Just off John Street, the bustling main street in the south-west Sydney suburb of Cabramatta, stands the ornate Freedom Gate. Built of white marble and teak and standing over five metres tall, the archway is adorned with tiles in a Chinese style. It bears a number of inscriptions. Spelled out in bold are 'Liberty' and 'Democracy', both of which are written in English, Chinese, Vietnamese, Khmer and Lao. At the Gate's centre, there is an exhortation: 'To rest in the highest excellence.' On its left pillar: 'To be renovative and integrate.' And on its right: 'To understand illustrious virtue.'

Quite apart from the strange syntax and elliptical meaning of the inscriptions – perhaps a mild case of 'Chinglish' – the Freedom Gate tells an instructive story about multiculturalism in Australia. When the archway was erected in the early 1990s, Cabramatta was considered the nation's drug capital, the undisputed home of organised Asian crime. The local state member of parliament at the time, John Newman, declared that criminals in the suburb should be deported 'back to the jungle' in Asia, where they belonged. Cabramatta was widely regarded as a ghetto, a troubled badland, an example of multicultural dysfunction. The shooting murder of Newman outside his home in 1994, and the subsequent conviction of Vietnamese community leader and local councillor Phuong Ngo, only seemed to confirm Cabramatta's unsavoury reputation.

It was a reputation that had much basis in reality, as I came to learn, growing up. For a number of years, from the 1980s to the 1990s, my family lived in Canley Vale, an adjoining suburb. My parents shopped in Cabramatta for groceries; we ate at its many restaurants. Although we later moved a few kilometres away to Bonnyrigg Heights, I still caught a bus most days to Cabramatta and then a train from the railway station to school. For most of my adolescent years, the Cabramatta I knew was a sketchy place. Drug deals brazenly took place on street corners. Junkies overdosed on bus stop benches and train station platforms. Parks and playgrounds were littered with used syringes. Footpaths were splattered with vomit. I would sometimes walk past friends from primary school, their eyes glazed over like young zombies' from their heroin addiction.

Almost two decades on, the suburb is in many ways beyond recognition. The drugs have disappeared, as have the gangs. Newman and Ngo are now largely forgotten names. The centre of Cabramatta is a thriving commercial precinct. Far from being a place even locals would avoid, the suburb is a tourist attraction. Brochures for visitors to Sydney celebrate Cabramatta as 'a taste of Asia'. On a typical Saturday, visitors are greeted by the frenetic activity you might associate with Ho Chi Minh City. The *pho* noodle houses are unfailingly busy. The bakeries, invariably called 'Hot Bread' shops, do a roaring trade in pork rolls. The strains of Vietnamese ballads blare from DVD stores. Shopping arcades are lined with fruit stalls stocked with coconuts, durians, jackfruits and mangoes. Walking along the footpaths requires one to negotiate old Vietnamese ladies in triangular straw hats selling rice sweets wrapped in banana leaves.

Yet far from being just a locale of exotic interest, Cabramatta has also been a success story of multicultural integration. To drive around Cabramatta and its surrounding suburbs is to discover neighbourhoods that have enjoyed a steady rise in house prices over the past two decades. The story is confirmed for anyone who makes the train journey from Cabramatta into central Sydney on your average weekday. Train carriages are filled with young professionals commuting to work, and university students on their way to morning lectures. If you pause to listen to the voices within the carriages, the sound is of an Australian English with the distinctive mark of south-west Sydney, bearing the residual tones and cadences of Chinese and Vietnamese. The tale is one of social mobility rather than of social disadvantage.

The mission of integration, emblazoned as it is on the Freedom Gate, is for the most part accomplished. It is for these reasons that I consider Cabramatta to be symbolic of our multicultural experience, and of the sometimes difficult journey that many immigrants have made from threatening stranger to fellow citizen. Just how this process works reflects not only an Australian model of immigrant settlement, but also a national expression of a civic philosophy.

A civic philosophy

To refer to multiculturalism as a civic philosophy may strike some people as unusual. In public debate, the word can exist as a kind of word association game that draws out people's ideological view of the world. For its supporters, multiculturalism is about the harmonious diversity of cultures, and the rejection of racism and conformity. For its critics, the concept is about cultural preservation, social segregation and the rejection of national unity. For some, multiculturalism is an umbrella term to describe a 'politics of difference' and the various claims for recognition made by ethnic or racial minorities, indigenous national groups, women, gays and lesbians.[1] Others see it as concerned more with immigrants and the question of social integration. It is rare to find agreement on what the concept means, let alone on whether it is a good or a bad thing. But in its various expressions, multiculturalism as a civic philosophy isn't the most common starting point. Yet it should be.

If there's an essence that defines multiculturalism, it is liberal citizenship. Clearly, it isn't about citizenship as it has been traditionally understood. Multiculturalism emerged as a reaction against an ideal of cultural homogeneity which has defined nationhood across most Western nation-states. Those who didn't belong to the dominant national group within a state were either to be assimilated into it or excluded from it altogether. A multicultural state is based on a different idea. Rather than assimilate or exclude differences, the state should recognise and accommodate cultural diversity. What this means in practice will vary, depending on the minority cultural group in question. For indigenous minority peoples, multicultural rights may mean the recognition of land rights or self-government rights; for immigrant groups, it may mean, among other things, the introduction of anti-discrimination laws or greater sensitivity to diversity in public institutions. Either way, a multicultural state involves some set of 'group-differentiated' rights or policies targeted at minority groups who have been traditionally excluded from the nation-state.[2]

Properly understood, multiculturalism isn't just about culture but is about a civic aspiration. In his seminal essay on identity, philosopher Charles Taylor reminds us that its novelty lies in demanding of us two different concepts of equality. There is equal dignity, Taylor wrote, which involves everyone as citizens enjoying the same basket of rights and immunities. Then there is the idea of equal recognition, which asks that we recognise 'the unique identity of this individual or group, their distinctiveness from everyone else'.[3] It is the latter concept of cultural recognition that marks out multiculturalism as an ideological development in liberalism. Just as all should enjoy equal civil and political rights, regardless of ethnicity or race, so all should enjoy a presumption that their cultural identities have value. In this sense, multiculturalism has been a 'child of liberal egalitarianism', though 'like any child, it is not simply a faithful reproduction of its parents'.[4]

This is reflected in the practical application of a multicultural approach. As a civic philosophy, it overturns the notion of state neutrality towards cultural groups. A multicultural state isn't bound by the idea that laws must be applied without any differentiation between members of a community, as a matter of impartiality. After all, to what extent can any state ever be neutral? All states inevitably bear the marks of the histories of their dominant or majority communities, at the very least through things such as the language in which official business is conducted or the days that are marked as official public holidays. That an Australian state conducts its affairs in the English language and has public holidays that align with Christian days of observance reflects a particular history that isn't neutral. The specific claim of multiculturalism is that neutrality is an impossible goal. Rather, the crucial values are fairness and equality. No rule or norm or convention in society should unjustly disadvantage citizens because of their backgrounds or beliefs.[5]

This may mean some revision of existing practices which enjoy the implied or explicit status of official neutrality. For example, in their review of cultural accommodation in French-speaking Quebec, the Bouchard-Taylor Commission in Canada recommended that officials relocate a crucifix that sits visibly above the chair of the president of Quebec's National Assembly (the equivalent of a state parliament), so as not to unjustly privilege the Christian faith in what should be a secular public space.[6] In other circumstances, a multicultural state may offer some differentiated treatment to minorities: it may allow a policeman of Sikh background to wear his turban in place of the usual standard issue hat, or set aside a time during the day for Muslim women to use a section of a public swimming pool. These are modest exemptions motivated by values of equality and fairness. Fair and equal treatment by the state needn't mean *identical* treatment.

The liberal democratic credentials of multiculturalism aren't universally accepted. Those who pursue the 'essentialist critique' warn against defining an individual by their cultural heritage.[7] 'All the ambiguity of multiculturalism', writes French philosopher Pascal Bruckner, 'proceeds from the fact that with the best intentions, it imprisons men, women, and children in a way of life and in traditions from which they often aspire to free themselves. The politics of identity in fact reaffirm difference at the very moment when we are trying to establish equality.'[8] Where we are too preoccupied with cultural identity, we may presume someone with, say, Indian heritage may end up being regarded as more 'Indian' than they actually like to be; we may end up judging people by something like their essential physical characteristics without any attention to their individual personality. Someone who works as a professional, enjoys rock music, watches sport, speaks French, and who also happens to bear Indian ancestry may end up being thought of as just 'Indian' and no more.

Multiculturalism would be hard to justify if it ended up 'essentialising' people in this way. Yet we shouldn't assume that it does. To endorse a multicultural approach is merely to accept that a person's cultural identity is tied to their dignity as a person; that a cultural identity provides some context within which an individual makes their choices about how to live their life. Thus understood, multiculturalism leaves room for a good deal of fluidity in how people come to exercise their cultural identification. Surveys conducted in Britain, for example, show that while those from immigrant backgrounds retain their cultural identities through generations, they don't necessarily participate in activities or behave in ways associated with their cultural group. Britons of an

Indian background, in the second and subsequent generations, mightn't wear Indian dress, or attend a temple or mosque, or even use an Indian language, but they nonetheless think of themselves as culturally Indian in many ways.[9] The point of multiculturalism isn't that anyone bearing some Indian lineage must, by virtue of that, identify as Indian. It is, rather, to allow for individuals to do so without being socially stigmatised.

Other critics of multiculturalism focus on another supposed flaw. Those who advance the 'solidarity critique' contend that multiculturalism can end up 'hollowing out' citizenship, by depriving it of any sense of a common good.[10] According to one proponent of this view, the historian James Curran, cultural diversity is 'the very opposite' of national unity. Multiculturalism, he argues, means that a community can only be characterised by its differences, since it cannot explain how 'the nation remains cohesive'.[11] In other words, a country may end up as an aggregation of tribes.

But, as noted in Chapter 1, multiculturalism's rejection of certain forms of unity doesn't amount to a rejection of unity altogether. This is a point that escapes historians such as Curran, along with his recent collaborator Stuart Ward. In their book *The Unknown Nation*, Curran and Ward argue that an Australian national identity has only truly enjoyed coherence and power when it was supported by 'British race patriotism'.[12] It is true that Australians for a long time conceived of themselves as British as much as Australian; it was natural for men of Robert Menzies's generation to dream about spending their final years in a cottage in the idyllic Kent countryside back in the 'mother country'. The mistake is to believe that anything other than this kind of race patriotism must be judged a failure. Within *The Unknown Nation*, one finds at play an ambivalent attitude to contemporary notions of an Australian civic culture. Even a civic culture based on Australian parliamentary democracy, drawing upon a British institutional inheritance, seems not enough to count as a foundation for national identity. Successive efforts by Australian prime ministers and governments to articulate an identity that is distinct from traditional notions of Britishness are hence quietly mocked by Curran and Ward. That wistful longing for the essence of race patriotism and the security of Empire remains; at least, that is the impression. It is perhaps a case of unacknowledged nostalgia.

Critics of multiculturalism can forget that national identities are much more dynamic than they may seem. They are the product of 'imagined communities'.[13] They evolve with time. It is simplistic to believe that nations could only have a genuine common identity where its members possess the same ancestry or ethnicity. To belong to a nation means that one belongs to a certain common culture, but any culture is necessarily dynamic (I will say more about what the content of a national culture must involve in Chapter 3). For instance, there is nothing bizarre about chicken tikka masala being considered England's national dish, or about the cappuccino being Australia's favourite hot beverage. Nor is it strange that people have hyphenated identities such as Irish-American or Italian-Australian or British-Muslim. Multiculturalism simply means that there's no one typical way for someone to belong to a national community. It is an affirmation of pluralism, but one firmly within the context of the nation. This doesn't mean that solidarity is impossible. As a civic philosophy, multiculturalism demands a different view of what constitutes a common bond among a people.

The retreat from multiculturalism

So far I've covered multiculturalism in theory, explaining how it stands up to the usual philosophical objections. But for many, the problem isn't so much the theory as the social and political reality. Haven't recent developments across Western liberal democracies proven multiculturalism to be a failure?

There is no question that the events of September 11 in 2001, and al-Qaeda-inspired terrorist attacks in Madrid and London, have heightened anxiety about immigration and social cohesion. There are concerns about multicultural permissiveness leading to so-called home-grown terrorism. Such worries haven't been confined to far-right extremist groups, but have been expressed by increasingly strident mainstream voices. For instance, the bestselling 2010 book *Deutschland schafft sich ab* (*Germany Abolishes Itself*) – which sparked a national debate about multiculturalism in Germany with its prediction that unassimilable Muslim immigrants would overrun the country – was written not by a fringe-dwelling scribbler but by a prominent Social Democrat politician and governor of the German reserve bank, Thilo Sarrazin.[14] Centre-right governments in Germany, France, Britain and the Netherlands have all declared the multicultural approach a failure. In Belgium and France, there have even been bans introduced on the wearing of burqas and niqabs in public places. The mood has shifted decidedly towards a firm reassertion of national cultural integrity. There appears to be an emerging consensus that multicultural policies have, to use the words of British Prime Minister David Cameron, 'encouraged different cultures to live separate lives, apart from each other and apart from the mainstream'.[15]

The European rejection of multiculturalism has prompted many here to declare that it is time for Australian governments to do the same. This has included some prominent public voices previously supportive of multiculturalism. Take conservative commentator Gerard Henderson, a consistent critic of Pauline Hanson in the 1990s and defender of multiculturalism in the aftermath of the Cronulla riots. Acknowledging that he was once 'critical of John Howard's apparent disdain for the concept', Henderson noted in early 2011 that 'on reflection, I am coming to the view that some of Howard's critique was essentially correct'. The likes of David Cameron and Angela Merkel, he argued, are 'correct in criticising multiculturalism and what it has become in Western Europe – namely, a focus on what divides democratic societies'. It is 'reasonable to assume' that multiculturalism would have such a negative effect here 'unless we adopt a muscular approach to the affirmation of democratic rights'.[16] *The Australian*'s long-standing foreign affairs editor Greg Sheridan, who assured readers in 1996 that 'there is nothing in multiculturalism that could cause any worry to any normal person', has made a similar reversal. Declaring the policy 'a failure', Sheridan contends that 'it's very unclear that the term made any positive contribution to the happy settlement of migrants'. If anything, he says, it has delayed the 'normalisation' of cultural diversity.[17]

The Henderson–Sheridan view has much in common with other contemporary conservative critiques of multiculturalism. These can be differentiated, it must be said, from Hansonist objections made in the late 1990s. Typically they aren't expressed in nationalistic terms of defending an Australian culture and identity against encroachments by ethnic minorities, particularly those from Asia. Rather, they are couched in language about social cohesion, the primacy of Western values and the need to resist unconditional tolerance of cultural differences. Writing in 2006, conservative columnist Janet Albrechtsen argued that multiculturalism ends up 'separating people according to culture and eschewing any criticism of minorities'. It 'rejects any expectation of integration and notions of core values' and 'promotes Australia as a series of Balkanised statelets'.[18] The same year, the then Treasurer Peter Costello derided a 'confused, mushy, misguided multiculturalism'. Warning that Australian values are 'not optional', Costello said that naturalised immigrants who failed to honour their pledge of allegiance to Australia should have their citizenship revoked. At one point, he drew an analogy between arriving in Australia as an immigrant and entering a mosque as a visitor. Just as it is customary to take off one's shoes as a sign of respect in a mosque, so immigrants should subscribe to certain values. Those who object to them shouldn't come to Australia, much as those who object to walking in their socks shouldn't enter a mosque.[19]

This take on multiculturalism's supposed civic deficiencies has gathered momentum since the Cronulla riot of December 2005. Some remember the Cronulla episode not so much for the violence of a 5000-strong mob targeting people of Middle Eastern appearance in the name of national pride as for how some minority groups have pushed Australia's Anglo-Celtic majority to the limits of their tolerance. As publisher Peter Ryan opined in the pages of *The Australian* shortly after the riot, 'indiscriminate immigration and the accompanying madness of multiculturalism' were to blame. In Ryan's view, what happened at Cronulla proved Geoffrey Blainey correct in his prediction that there would be racial strife in the nation's streets.[20] Certainly, a good deal of media commentary was devoted to exploring the source of tensions between primarily Lebanese-Australian youths and locals in Sutherland Shire. Of particular concern was the long-running grievance against Lebanese-Australian youths, whom locals believed were taking over Cronulla beach, whether through their games of football on the sand or their aggressive sexual pursuit of white Anglo-Celtic women. The spark for the riot was an altercation between some Lebanese-Australian youths and lifesavers a week earlier, which was widely publicised in tabloid newspapers and talkback radio in Sydney.[21]

There was a striking quality about much of the post-Cronulla analysis, however. The mere suggestion that jingoism may have contributed to the Cronulla riot was, according to many conservatives, an act of complicity in cultural relativism and political correctness. Multiculturalism meant that political leaders could never openly criticise members of immigrant communities; it would only be 'mainstream Australia' that would be censured.[22] Conservative writers focused disproportionately on the acts of retaliation by Lebanese-Australian youths. *Sydney Morning Herald* journalist Paul Sheehan, for example, brushed aside the violence at Cronulla as

hol-fuelled, random and spontaneous' mob hysteria.
lis was quite unlike 'the response from the hard men
in Lakemba, Punchbowl and Bankstown', which was 'co-
ordinated, armed, premeditated and took the violence
to another level'.[23] The alleged failure of multiculturalism didn't just mean that some minorities were beyond
criticism. It also meant something dangerous had been
unleashed on the nation's streets. In his book *Girls Like
You*, Sheehan explicitly linked the Cronulla riot to the
series of gang rapes perpetrated by Bilal Skaf and others:
both represented how Muslim males were 'cultural time-
bombs' in a liberal society.[24]

Conservatives weren't the only ones who believed
that Cronulla highlighted the trouble with multiculturalism. Anthropologist Ghassan Hage, arguably the country's most original critic of nationalism, also declared
that the episode revealed a contemporary crisis. Hage's
thesis is admittedly complex. His starting point is that
multicultural policy is based on ensuring that cultural
diversity exists only so as to enrich a broader, 'white'
national culture into which immigrants can integrate.
Multiculturalism effectively means a 'white multiculturalism', a disguised form of cultural assimilation. For
Hage, the significance of Cronulla lies in the apparent
emergence of what he calls the 'ungovernable' Muslim
minority. The Lebanese-Australian youths who were at
the centre of the episode radically defied the terms of
the 'multicultural-assimilationist apparatus'.[25] The prob-

lem wasn't that they lived outside an Australian culture. It was that they were too comfortable with their cultural differences and weren't the kind of Australians others wanted them to be:

> What is behind the claims that Lebanese youths were unintegrated was the fear that they seemed *overintegrated*. For people who are so different they were too integrated for their own good: they had no sense of their assumed marginality: arrogant. 'We don't expect you to act like this on the beach,' the assimilationists and multiculturalists were screaming in unison. 'Can't you be a bit shy for God's sake! You should feel like hiding your feelings when you are desiring an Aussie chick on the beach in *this* way.' ... It is in this that the Lebanese-Australian youths exhibited their ungovernability in the face of the multicultural-assimilationist duo that were often deployed *in tandem* to ensure the integration of people in Australian culture.[26]

Cronulla has undoubtedly shaped a good deal of the retreat from multiculturalism, although global developments have perhaps been the more dominant influence. In the cases of Henderson and Sheridan, there is an extrapolation from the supposed problems of multiculturalism in Europe: the Europeans have said that multiculturalism there has failed; therefore, it is only a matter of time before it fails here too. Yet does it make sense to draw clear-cut lessons about Australian multiculturalism's supposed failure from European experience?

The actual source of concern with the European model of multiculturalism needs clarification. What seems to have prompted the change of heart from former defenders of Australian multiculturalism is a particular concern with growing Muslim minorities, some of whose practices and identities are allegedly incompatible with the values of Western democracy.[27] For Henderson, while multiculturalism in Australia worked well throughout the 1970s, 1980s and 1990s, this was no guarantee that it will work now. With the rise of radical Islam, there is 'a situation where a small minority of Islamists reject the West while choosing to live within Western societies, where they enjoy economic, political and religious freedoms along with health and social security benefits'.[28] Sheridan similarly identifies Muslim immigrant populations as the source of social disharmony in Europe. Citing anecdotal experience of antisocial behaviour and jihadi culture on the streets of Lakemba in Sydney's south-west – his evidence includes witnessing youths of Middle Eastern appearance spitting in the face of old white ladies – he argues that Australia might easily be similarly heading towards 'a European future' of failed integration.[29] Albeit using the term in a different way to Hage, Henderson and Sheridan seem to concur with the diagnosis of an 'ungovernable' Muslim minority.

It is true that a substantial number of Australians today regard the word 'multiculturalism' as a synonym for Muslim immigration.[30] Surely, however, this is a category error. This isn't to deny that integrating immigrants from Muslim backgrounds is part of any contemporary multicultural equation; clearly it is, and jihadist extremism is incompatible with liberal democracy. But some perspective is needed. If multiculturalism is concerned with the settlement of immigrants, and more broadly with how cultural diversity can be reconciled with a national identity, then Muslim immigrants form only part of the overall picture. Australia has a relatively small Muslim population of around 476 000 (or 2.2 per cent of the national population), according to the 2011 Census.[31] The majority of immigrants who arrive in Australia now come from Asia, and aren't Muslim in background. If multiculturalism were an abject failure as public policy, as suggested, then the symptoms should be present among other groups, in addition to Muslim immigrants.

This isn't something that those who have proclaimed a crisis of multiculturalism have demonstrated. While endorsing the stances of Merkel and Cameron, Henderson acknowledges that 'in Australia and the US, multiculturalism has not had such a negative effect'.[32] Sheridan acknowledges that Australia, the US and Canada have in fact experienced impressive stability and cohesion as nations of immigration. In his view, Europe's problems seem mainly to do with the fact that Muslim immigrant populations count for a larger percentage of the total population than they do here. The differences seem to have little to do with multiculturalism, as he admits himself.

The likes of Henderson and Sheridan have undergone curious, ill-founded conversions to the anti-multiculturalism brigade. Their claims that multiculturalism will lead Australia to sleepwalk into European-style troubles are offered with little supporting evidence. It is as if invoking 'Muslims' and 'Europe', and the apparently unimpeachable wisdom of Merkel, Sarkozy and Cameron, were enough. But to say that the problems faced by some European countries signal that the same problems exist here is akin to saying that a design flaw in an Audi or a Peugeot means that one's Holden will possess an identical flaw. It doesn't hold up. We shouldn't draw the wrong lessons from Europe.

How Australia is different

Critics of multiculturalism often fail to recognise that the experience of integration around the world reveals some national variation. The Australian version of multiculturalism is different from that of other countries. Of course, it isn't quite right to say that the experience of Australian multiculturalism is unique. It does share a number of qualities with the versions practised in Canada, and to a lesser extent the US. While they are settler nations,

Australia, Canada and the US once adopted an assimilationist approach to immigration that was intolerant of diversity. Just as Australia had a White Australia policy and the infamous dictation test, aimed at keeping out 'Asiatics', both Canada and the US had legislation directed at restricting immigrants from Asia (and also southern and eastern Europeans in some periods). Since the 1960s and 1970s this has been replaced, in each of these countries, by a pluralistic approach to immigration and integration. Racially discriminatory admissions criteria have been dropped. Immigrants, regardless of their origin, have been granted equal rights in all spheres of society without being expected to abandon their cultural affiliations. The guiding idea within multicultural countries such as Australia, Canada and the US has effectively been one of citizenship: anyone who arrives in the country and settles permanently should be given a path towards becoming a full member of the community.

Even so, we can distinguish between different multiculturalisms as practised by the classic immigrant-settler nations of Australia, Canada and the US. Most notably, the US has never practised an official multiculturalism, opting instead for a more laissez-faire approach. The US government has never provided systematic government assistance with settlement through language classes and improved access to government services. Nor has it actively supported the maintenance of immigrant ethnic cultures. Where multiculturalism has been most influential in the US has been in education, with the amendment of school and university curricula to reflect greater diversity. Even between Australia and Canada, the two archetypal examples of multiculturalism, there are noticeable differences. The Canadian experience is complicated by the bilingual nature of Canadian society and by the claims of a substantial section of Quebecois for national self-government. Multicultural expression has existed within the context of a bilingual Canada, and with due recognition of Quebec as a 'distinct society'. In other words, where diverse immigrants are integrated, it has historically been into *either* an English-speaking Canada or a Francophone Canada represented by Quebec.[33]

Australian multiculturalism has been more straightforward. As outlined in Chapter 1, Australian governments have always balanced the endorsement of cultural diversity with affirmations of national unity. Any such unity hasn't been burdened by official bilingualism and the weight of minority nationalism. Since the mid-1980s, a citizenship model of multiculturalism has operated explicitly. The freedom to express one's cultural identity and heritage has been formalised as a right – a cultural right in addition to civil, political and social rights – but this has been balanced by civic responsibilities. The record of immigrant integration in Australia since the 1970s reveals that it is unambiguously a journey of citizenship, in theory and in practice.

Australian governments have been exemplary in encouraging new arrivals to take out formal membership of the national community. Among Organisation for Economic Co-operation and Development (OECD) countries, Australia has a high 'take-up' rate of citizenship from immigrants – an estimated 80 per cent of immigrants with more than ten years of residence have chosen to adopt Australian citizenship.[34]

The integration of immigrants in Australia has been an overwhelming success. It is no mean feat that dramatic changes in the ethnic and cultural composition of Australia have taken place without widespread social disruption. At the end of the Second World War, Australia's population was overwhelming Anglo-Celtic, with well over 90 per cent of the population being of Anglo-Celtic stock. Today around 25 per cent of Australians were born overseas, with close to 45 per cent having at least one parent who was an immigrant. While Smith remains the most common surname in the country, names such as Chen, Kim, Singh and Nguyen aren't far behind.[35] Such conspicuous diversity, in many ways inconceivable for Australians who grew up in the 1940s or 1950s, has for the most part been received with tolerance, understanding and goodwill. We can compare Australia's record with, for instance, the United Kingdom. There, the influx of immigrants from its former colonies in South Asia, the Caribbean and East Africa from the 1950s through to the 1970s has been accompanied by considerable social tensions. Race riots in Britain, many occurring between members of far-right extremist groups and immigrant minorities, have been a regular occurrence. Notting Hill in 1958, Lewisham in 1977, St Pauls in 1980, Brixton in 1981, Bradford and Oldham in 2001, Birmingham in 2005 – these are only some of the more notable examples over the years. By contrast, Australia has been a model of social harmony and stability. It is one reason why an episode like Cronulla has rightly prompted such widespread introspection. For most of the past 50 years Australia's record has been exceptional.

And if one regards the performance of immigrants and their children in education and in employment as fair indicators, Australia seems to be faring very well. Historically, immigrants from non-English-speaking backgrounds have been more likely to occupy the lower rungs of the workforce, reflecting the role of immigrants in industries such as manufacturing and construction. Even today, they still have worse employment outcomes than native-born Australians and those from English-speaking backgrounds; many highly skilled immigrants end up accepting jobs that don't match their educational qualifications in their home countries.[36] But there has never been a numerically significant underclass of immigrants whose members suffer permanent high employment and little prospect of economic improvement. Australian immigrants have work participation rates that are above the national average.

In any case, the truest measure of integration should be generational; the process takes time. Take the case of Indochinese refugees and immigrants in Cabramatta and south-west Sydney. A little more than a decade ago, they were considered by many to have constituted a failure of integration; today, they are regarded as a success story. In broader terms, it is striking that the children of immigrants outperform children of native-born Australians. Australia is one of the very few OECD countries – Canada and the US are other notable countries – where the children of immigrants constitute a higher proportion of people in highly skilled occupations than the children of natives.[37]

First- and second-generation Australians increasingly dominate classrooms in academically selective government high schools, not to mention enrolments in the law and medicine faculties of the nation's most elite universities. The nurseries of the country's elite aren't impenetrable bastions, with admission a birthright. Unlike other countries, our universities haven't typically had to introduce special policies or affirmative action to ensure adequate diversity in their intakes. Under-representation of the children of immigrants isn't a problem. Compare the diversity of our top universities, for example, with the University of Oxford, which in 2011 admitted a mere 32 black students for undergraduate study – the highest total in a decade.[38] Or with the prestigious École National d'Administration, France's leading finishing school for government officials, where the child of a North African immigrant would be an exotic specimen among the children of Parisian upper-middle-class privilege.[39]

To what extent does this demonstrate that Australian multiculturalism has ensured that immigrants and their children are well integrated? Some of it certainly reflects the fact that Australian governments have made an effort to attract skilled immigrants since the late 1970s (although the immigration intake during the 1970s and 1980s included a significant proportion who arrived on family reunion or humanitarian schemes).[40] But it isn't just the composition of immigrants that explains why integration has worked. Policies relating to settlement, and access and equity, have played an important role in equipping immigrants to participate in Australian society. It seems only logical to posit that where immigrants feel that they belong to a new society, and feel accepted for who they are and where they come from, they will have a better chance of doing well. Multicultural policies have provided a platform for immigrants and their children to succeed.

To gauge the impact of official multiculturalism, consider those liberal democracies that have opted for a different approach. Indeed, what has been described as 'multiculturalism' in Europe is more often than not something rather different. Most notably, when Germans refer to their failed attempt at 'multikulti', they aren't referring to the kind of multicultural citizenship that has been practised here – Germany has never endorsed an official policy involving the public recognition of cultural differences, and involving dedicated settlement and integration policies. It makes little sense to say that multiculturalism has failed in Germany – it was never adopted in the first place.

What was implemented in Germany from the 1960s until recently, when West Germany took in large numbers of immigrants (mainly from Turkey) to fill labour shortages, has been a form of 'differential exclusion'.[41] While accepting immigrants as members of civil society, partially integrated into the labour market, Germany clung to an Old World view of citizenship. Immigrants were never welcomed as arrivals who would become future citizens, but were tolerated as guest workers who were expected to return home once their work was done. It wasn't until 2000 that German nationality law adopted the principle of *jus soli*, allowing those born in the country to parents without native ancestry to claim citizenship. This helps explain why immigrants have struggled to integrate into German society. Compared to the situation here in Australia, the deficiencies are dramatic. Unemployment among working-age immigrants is twice as high as that for the rest of the working-age population. Whereas 20 per cent of Germans 'without a migration background' possess a university degree, this is true for only 10 per cent of German citizens of Turkish background, and only 2 per cent of resident Turkish nationals. One-third of German citizens of Turkish origin possess no qualifications beyond high school, compared to 12 per cent for ethnic Germans.[42]

France has also been a country falsely diagnosed with failed multiculturalism when it never adopted it. But whereas Germany had a clearly exclusionary model of nationhood, France has had a rigidly assimilationist one. This has been inclusive in one sense: the French republic has always been willing to grant citizenship to immigrants and their children. It is just that the French state has never been willing to make any accommodation of cultural diversity. The republican model considers all citizens to be equally French without any differentiation.[43] Thus, the French census symbolically declines to classify people by their ethnicity or religious affiliation. French authorities are uncompromising about any visible expression of cultural differences. Bans on headscarves in schools and, more recently, on the wearing of burqas and niqabs in all public places are but examples of French republican absolutism. Such assimilationist policies have been regarded as providing cover for institutionalised racism in French society. There is a deep feeling of resentment and alienation felt by many French youths of North African background. At times this has exploded into widespread civil unrest, most notoriously in 2005, when rioting in the 'banlieues' (suburbs) in Paris and other major cities prompted the French government to declare a state of emergency that lasted more than three months.

Nation-building

There is another set of comparisons that illustrates the particular character of the Australian multicultural approach. Some countries have adopted an official multiculturalism, but have failed to strike the proper balance between cultural diversity and national unity. There are some examples of multicultural integration regimes – not just regimes of differential exclusion and assimilation mislabelled – that have failed to emphasise the limits of tolerating cultural differences and the unifying aspects of national identity. For example, while Britain and the Netherlands may be correctly cited as countries that have adopted an official multiculturalism, they haven't defined their policies as successive Australian governments have done.

As sociologist Paul Scheffer has argued in his book *Immigrant Nations*, multiculturalism in the Netherlands has been distinctively shaped by what he calls a Dutch 'culture of avoidance'. Dutch society has historically been defined by its 'ability to blunt sharp edges'. Its traditional 'pillarisation' regime, which allowed for the parallel co-existence of a number of social groups or 'pillars', was a celebrated model of religious and political tolerance.[44]

Yet, when applied to the integration of immigrants, this ethos of 'each keeping to its own' proved highly questionable. Dutch multicultural policy, for example, never prioritised among its immigrant arrivals the importance of acquiring the Dutch language. Many *children* of immigrants failed, and still fail, to develop full command of Dutch. Compare this to Australian multiculturalism, which has made explicit an expectation that all immigrants accept English as the national language, and which has included language training as a key component of settlement policies. A political culture of 'avoidance' and moderation, moreover, has spilled over into a form of cultural self-negation. Prominent Dutch historians such as the late Ernst Kossmann wrote that the country had 'no use' for 'pompous terms like national identity'.[45] Such indifference hasn't aided the management of cultural diversity. Insofar as the approach of pillarisation worked in accommodating religious and political differences, it did so because it was accompanied by a certain Dutch nationalism; the advent of multiculturalism broke this link.

British multiculturalism, meanwhile, is complicated by its relationship with postcolonial waves of immigration. A culturally diverse Britain in the 20th century only came about after the Second World War and the formation of the Commonwealth after decolonisation. Nationality laws introduced in 1948 rendered every citizen of the Commonwealth a British subject and permitted them to settle in Britain (thus retaining the freedom of movement that had existed in the Empire). Unexpectedly for British policymakers, this led to high numbers of immigrants arriving from the former colonies – predominantly, at first, from the Caribbean. The phenomenon of postwar immigration from the Commonwealth was a peculiar development: it was 'as much a migration within an extended polity as between polities, even though some of the imperial territories had recently acquired independence'.[46]

The history behind Britain's cultural diversity helps to explain a number of features of its multiculturalism. In the first place, the imperial hangover has meant that social integration in Britain hasn't emphasised a well-defined, unifying civic identity. The fact that there had been an Empire for so long, on which the sun famously never set, meant that British governments never believed that explicit expressions of a collective identity were needed. The Empire, being what it was, spoke for itself. Since most of Britain's new arrivals came from Commonwealth nations, with strong cultural ties to the Empire, the issue of a cohesive British identity wasn't a problem. Many immigrants, especially from the Caribbean, went to Britain believing they were being called to the 'mother country' to assist in its reconstruction after the war (many would find that their enthusiasm wasn't necessarily shared by Britons). Australian multiculturalism, being a response to planned immigration, has always been closely tied to an infrastructure of settlement policies and services, but this hasn't been the case in Britain. Neither has the language of citizenship featured strongly in British approaches to citizenship: after all, many postwar immigrants were British *subjects*.

The result of all this has been that British multi-culturalism, like its Dutch counterpart, has lacked a nation-building logic. Multiculturalism in Britain has always been primarily expressed in terms of tolerance and race relations. Where official statements about multiculturalism have been offered, they appear ambivalent about an overarching British identity to which all citizens could subscribe. Hence, the much-cited report of the Commission on the Future of Multi-Ethnic Britain, *The Future of Multi-Ethnic Britain*, defined Britain as a 'community of communities' – language which suggested that Britain could be understood as a collection of groups without something in common.[47] As notable critics of British multiculturalism have argued, it veers towards emphasising the relative importance of communities over individuals and encouraging 'a fragmentary perception of the demands of living in a desegregated Britain'. This danger of 'plural monoculturalism' is particularly pronounced given the historic pattern of high residential concentrations of immigrant communities.[48] Where race riots have taken place, the locations have almost inevitably been those places with significant numbers of unemployed or alienated members of minority communities.

Placing the Australian experience into this international context underlines the special achievement of our multiculturalism. Far from being a failure, it has succeeded. And it has succeeded because it has been a policy aimed at civic integration and conducted as an exercise in nation-building.

Yet too often when the case is made for policies endorsing cultural diversity, the civic dimension of the argument is omitted. It seems easier to convey either the lifestyle or economic benefits of diversity – the contribution of immigrants and their descendants to Australian cuisine, say, or to the Australian economy. The trouble occurs when these arguments are relied upon without the context of a bigger picture. When used on its own, the lifestyle argument ends up trivialising diversity, implying that we should value minority cultures only insofar as they can enrich ours. What should happen, then, if Australians don't like Finnish or Nigerian or Kazakh cuisine? Reliance on the economic argument, on the other hand, implies that we shouldn't welcome immigrants who don't provide an obvious economic benefit, or that we shouldn't extend the welcome beyond when they're needed by the economy. The problem in both cases is that they divorce the recognition of diversity from the ends of citizenship. Multiculturalism as a policy is about ensuring that every citizen, regardless of their background, has the opportunity to fulfil their individual potential and contribute to the life of the Australian community. It isn't about lifestyle or economics as such. It is ultimately about a fair go, and about strengthening the Australian nation.

This points to one problem with much of the

contemporary language of culture and identity in Australian debate. Many of those sympathetic to cultural diversity regard the very idea of nation-building as anathema. The very mention of the words 'nation' and 'citizenship' can trigger suggestions either of white settler racism or of disguised assimilation.[49] It is believed that a celebration of diversity must be about transcending national identity and affirming a global humanity. Going down this path of repudiating nationhood and nationality does more harm than good, for it denies that multiculturalism has given nation-building a pluralistic form – that it has ensured citizenship is no longer a device of exclusion. It fails to honour multiculturalism as it has actually been practised in Australia, and it invites critics to depict it as merely a vehicle for progressive self-loathing. When defenders of cultural diversity reject multicultural nation-building they commit the equivalent of intellectual surrender.

3

How racist is this country?

It is a balmy night, on the eve of Australia Day, 2010. In Canberra's Federation Mall, just outside Parliament House, Patrick McGorry has just been named Australian of the Year. A free concert, part of the official celebrations, is getting underway before a mall that is awash with blue. The majority of the youthful concertgoers are wearing the Australian flag one way or another. Many wear it draped over their shoulders or have fashioned it into a sarong. As I wade my way through the growing crowd I feel like I'm navigating a sea of national pride.

It isn't until I'm driving away from parliament, however, that I experience my biggest dose of flag-waving patriotism. Out of the corner of my eye I see a young blonde-haired woman caped in a flag, leaning out the back window of the car alongside. She is yelling, 'Go home!' and making slit-eyed gestures at me – a tribute to my Asian ancestry. Her companions laugh and jeer.

Figuring that a civilised conversation is out of the question I respond with my own one-fingered salutes and robust compliments. Two of the blonde's friends in the car, both male, respond in turn as we wind around one of Canberra's circuitous roads – like chariots in the Colosseum, wheel to wheel. And then we come to a stop at a red light together. 'Why don't you come out and say that?' one challenges me. For a moment I consider testing my courage. Then the lights turn green. The other car speeds off into the distance.

Such episodes are enough to convince many of the perils of patriotism. They would say Barry Humphries was right when he quipped that, 'Xenophobia is love of Australia.'[1] That may well be true of many self-described patriots, but a love of country needn't be expressed as a desire to exclude others. It can be a humble and generous sentiment. You can be devoted to Australia and wish to see it do well, without beating your breast or telling others to 'Love it or leave it'. Patriotism can be an expression of civic virtue, of a desire to improve one's tradition and community.[2] But it clearly isn't always understood this way. Given the resurgence of national pride during the past decade or so, it is worth reflecting upon whether there has also been an accompanying increase in racism.

This is one tension that exists within today's multicultural Australia. Obviously, things have changed since the days of the White Australia policy and cultural assimilation. Laws have been passed to outlaw discrimination against citizens on the basis of ethnicity or race. Official multiculturalism welcomes the expression of cultural diversity as a right of citizenship. Diversity is widely accepted as an ordinary and positive feature of everyday Australian society.[3] Surveys consistently show that close to two-thirds of Australians would agree with propositions like 'Australia should be a multicultural society' or 'Immigrants have enriched the Australian way of life'.[4] And yet many would say that Australia remains incorrigibly racist. At the very least, as prominent neuro-surgeon Charlie Teo observed in his widely reported Australia Day address in 2012, 'Racism still exists in Australian culture today'.[5] Somewhere between 10 to 15 per cent of Australians have experienced discrimination in the past 12 months because of their skin colour, ethnic origin or religion.[6]

We shouldn't be surprised by the persistence of racism. For two centuries racism was a conspicuous feature of Australian society, guided as it was by an ideal of white, British nationhood. Any project of multicultural nation-building remains incomplete. As I mentioned in the previous chapter, some observers would ask whether 'nation-building' is itself the problem. Some contend that multicultural policy has the effect of masking discrimination and prejudice by placing an Anglo-Celtic culture at the core of Australian national identity, while quarantining immigrants and 'ethnic' cultures to its periphery.[7] Whereas conservatives believe multiculturalism has given immigrant minorities too much power and privilege, such cosmopolitan critics believe it has fooled us into believing in a fantasy of cultural progress. This thesis warrants closer attention. It is true, after all, that the policy of multiculturalism was introduced in the 1970s when the challenge of immigrant diversity was confined to predominantly European immigrants and cultures.

The critical question is whether Australian multiculturalism has since adapted itself to a diversity which is much more profound than its original architects anticipated. Under scrutiny here is nothing less than the robustness of the 'citizenship model' I have outlined in the previous two chapters. Multiculturalism can only be judged a success to the extent that Australians of minority ethnic and cultural backgrounds are able to imprint themselves into Australian life. While we are fond of saying that diversity is now a part of everyday Australia, there is a danger of premature self-congratulation. Multicultural policies have been successful in ensuring a well-integrated national community, but have they done enough also to transform hearts and minds in Australian society? Have they done enough to transform our national institutions? The extent to which racism exists will speak volumes about the precise scale of the Australian achievement.

The trouble with racism

Levelling the charge of racism in Australia isn't something to be done lightly. It tends to provoke strong, vehement denials. Those who make the accusation must prepare themselves for the inevitable response that what is perceived as racial intolerance might actually be more accurately described as racial insensitivity, something reflecting neither hate nor sinister malice, but a tactless and mischievous Aussie sense of humour.[8] Any offence caused, so the logic goes, should be forgiven as misunderstanding or harmless clumsiness. Perhaps that is one reason why a public figure such as Pauline Hanson, after what could only be described as a highly divisive political career, could be reinvented as an entertainment celebrity cavorting in reality television programs. No self-respecting member of a liberal democratic society likes to think they could be guilty of bigotry. There are few things more comforting to the national psyche than to be reassured that racism is a problem that exists in other, far-away places and not at home. When, for instance, the Cronulla riot of 2005 took place, John Howard could have denounced the episode as a contemptible incident with a clear racist edge, as plainly there was. Instead, he declared that the episode revealed 'no underlying racism' in Australian society.

It was a disappointing note for a prime minister to strike, given the nature of the riot and the events leading up to it. Consider the text of one SMS that circulated among many of those who would eventually take part in the riot of 11 December: 'This Sunday every Fucking Aussie in the Shire, get down to North Cronulla to help support Leb and wog bashing day ... Bring your mates down and let's show them this is our beach and they're never welcome back.'[9] Or consider the comments of Sydney broadcaster Alan Jones in the week leading up to the riot: he suggested inviting bikie gangs to participate in a 'community show of force' against 'Lebanese thugs'. According to Jones, 'it would be worth the price of admission to watch these cowards scurry back onto the train for the return trip to their lairs ... Australians old and new shouldn't have to put up with this scum.'[10] Such outbursts were enough to earn Jones an official rebuke from the Australian Communications and Media Authority for breaching its code of practice on racial vilification.

Howard's stance on Cronulla was opportunistic pandering at its worst (although the response of then opposition leader Kim Beazley could also be criticised for not being forthright enough). While he criticised the 'extreme elements' at work in the riot, Howard refused to acknowledge there was any significant problem of racism that required addressing. In doing so, he disowned the aggressors of Cronulla but not the attitudes that produced them.[11] More than this, he signalled that any suggestion of racism should be construed as a judgement about an 'underlying' quality in the national character. The ultimate effect of Howard's response to Cronulla has been to make it harder to raise any allegation of racism in public debate. What may look like racial discrimination or violence is just bad or stupid behaviour mislabelled; it couldn't possibly be racist, because that would amount to calling the essential decency of each and every Australian into question.

An absolutist response to racism also exists in the opposite form: there are many who hastily interpret everything as in some way racist or aimed at confirming a national racial hierarchy. At times this form of perpetual critique can lead to contrived absurdity. Like the boy who cried wolf, those who label anything and everything racist can end up not being credible voices at all. Take cultural theorist Suvendrini Perera, who in 2010 argued that the opening days of that year's election campaign was based on the reproduction of the white racial order of the Australian nation-state. The smoking gun for her was that Prime Minister Julia Gillard had been kissing white babies at the start of the election campaign. In one of the broadcasted images of Gillard campaigning in the suburban heartland, she had been 'garbed all in white', kissing an 'especially robust' baby (which was white). Treasurer and newly promoted Deputy Prime Minister Wayne Swan also happened to stand beside Gillard, looking on. All of this apparently added up to a political affirmation of the white Australian heterosexual family.[12]

The truth lies somewhere between these two poles. That racism exists is surely indisputable; it is just that we can't reduce all things to race. But what exactly do we mean by race and racism? This isn't as straightforward a question as it may seem. The case of Pauline Hanson offers a good illustration. While Hanson advanced a view of Asian immigration and multiculturalism which many considered to be racist, she consistently asserted that they weren't. In her maiden speech in 1996, for instance, Hanson insisted, 'I am not a racist by any definition of that word ... I am not opposed to any person or group because of their race, colour or national or ethnic origin. I do not think that anyone is superior or inferior to anyone else because of their origin or background.' Indeed, this was one defence often raised on Hanson's behalf: her arguments didn't rely so much on notions of Asians having certain racial characteristics, or being inferior, as they did on ideas about the supposed *cultural* effects of Asian immigration. As she infamously put it, the problem with Australia being swamped by Asians was that Asians 'have their own culture and religion, form ghettos and do not assimilate'.

There is one sense in which Hanson may have a case for pleading that she shouldn't be described as racist: she didn't subscribe to the kind of 'scientific' theories about race that were popularised in the late 19th century in Europe and America. As put forward by social Darwinists at the time, these theories were based on ideas about races as biologically distinct entities, distinguished by different phenotypical features such as skin colour. These various races belonged to a natural hierarchy of intelligence (with white or European races being the most superior). Such theories have long since been discredited. Natural and social scientists confirm there is no biological basis for believing that 'races' exist: they are merely social constructions. Morally speaking, particularly after the end of the Second World War and the horrors of Nazism, ideologies of race have been regarded as abhorrent – as part of colonial justifications of the conquest, exploitation and even extermination of peoples. Australia has been influenced by this development. The end of the White Australia policy led to race becoming seemingly eliminated from the political vocabulary.

And yet, we continue to speak of 'race' and 'racism'. Many people continue to believe that others belong to a specific race, and such beliefs shape their view of social identity.[13] The discrediting of quasi-scientific racism does mean that it is rare to hear anyone but the most extreme speak about the hierarchy of races. But this doesn't mean that there isn't prejudice, bigotry and discrimination against people on the basis of their ethnic, cultural and religious identities. The motivating factor behind such behavior is less likely to be a belief in racial superiority than it is fear of difference or anxiety about change. And, increasingly, what we would ordinarily think of as racist sentiment is bound up with notions about culture rather than biology. As racism scholar Jon Stratton explains, 'where previously race operated as a reductive concept and was thought to determine culture, now culture is the more privileged term and race is thought to be a signifier of culture'. That is to say, race exists as a way of classifying culture. This constitutes what sociologists have termed the 'new racism' or 'cultural racism'.[14] Contemporary expressions of racism tend to be based on the belief that a particular culture is incompatible with a mainstream way of life or national identity. Race is now the quality that marks supposedly abhorrent cultural differences. The new racism builds on physical features such as skin colour a set of negative stereotypes based on perceived cultural traits. Culture has come to be conceived as a fixed property of ethnic or religious groups, and transformed into something bearing a 'pseudobiological' character.[15]

Anti-Muslim sentiment is perhaps the most prevalent form of racialised cultural hostility today. Consider some submissions made by individuals to a recent Commonwealth parliamentary inquiry into multiculturalism (whose final report was yet to be released at the time of writing).[16] Among the hundreds of written submissions were scores of citizens who identified Muslims as posing a special threat to Australian society. Many provide considered reflections about their response to cultural diversity. Frequently it is the voice of cultural loss. But many of the submissions contain sentiments that could be considered symptomatic of 'cultural racism'. One citizen from Sydney, who identifies herself as 'just your typical traditional Aussie who loves her country', reports that 'I hate my area, I feel like an outsider'. Of particular concern is 'the Islamic culture/way of life', which in her view now dominates her local area, but 'is not what Australia is about'. As she puts it, 'I see too much moving away from Australian tradition and culture and becoming something that is not "typically Aussie" ... If you are lucky enough to settle here I say that you must embrace us, our people, our Heritage, our way of life, our values, ethics and morals, our culture.'[17] Another citizen submits that 'I have without exception found the Muslim person to be a social misfit'. Muslims are 'disproportionately represented in drugs and virtually every branch of crime' and don't 'fit in a free society'. The Muslim 'belongs back in the Middle East where he can practice his hatred and horrible culture'.[18] Another, from rural Victoria, wrote that 'Moslems will eventually destroy our way of life and what little Australian culture we have remaining'.[19]

Such sentiments clearly involve negative stereotypes of Muslims and those from the Middle East. The stereotypes entertained by the people quoted above indicate they're likely to believe that anyone who looks like a Muslim will be a bearer of a certain culture – one suspects they mightn't necessarily be aware of, say, the difference between a Lebanese-Australian Muslim and an Egyptian-Australian Coptic Christian. In turn, such a predisposition can express itself in acts of discrimination, whether that is on the basis of ethnicity or religion. In this case, it is apparent that much of the cultural prejudice against Muslims is held by Australians of Anglo-Celtic background. But prejudice and discrimination are just as real when they come from those from minority immigrant backgrounds. When, for example, reports emerged of a spate of 'curry bashings' perpetrated against members of the Indian community in the western Sydney suburb of Harris Park in 2009, it turned out that white Anglo-Celtic Australians weren't the culprits: Australians of Middle Eastern (primarily Lebanese) background were in fact to blame.[20] Those familiar with the experience of newly arrived African refugees in Melbourne suggest that incidents of anti-African racism often involve people from immigrant backgrounds.

There is some truth, then, in the saying that 'everyone is a racist' – something revealed in psychological studies of 'implicit associations'.[21] But regardless of who perpetrates it, more often than not racism is an exercise in domination. It subjects others to stereotyping as members of an ethnic or national group with some essential, unchangeable qualities. Since our identities are partly shaped by cultural recognition – by whether others acknowledge our cultural distinctiveness and worth – people can suffer where there is 'non-recognition' or 'mis-recognition'. This occurs when people or society mirror back to them a demeaning or contemptible picture of themselves. Such episodes can involve a form of social oppression.[22]

We should be clear about exactly where any harm lies. The issue isn't simply about someone offending your cultural identity. As attacks on Indian students in Melbourne during 2009 and the Cronulla riot of 2005 demonstrate, racism can involve physical violence; recent reports of assaults on international students from China seem to indicate that episodes of racist violence, particularly in our major cities, aren't as isolated as we may think. Yet, even short of assault, episodes of racism can affect someone's physical and mental well-being.[23] Prejudice and discrimination are barriers to fair treatment and equal opportunity in the workplace. They harm an individual's ability to participate as a citizen in the community. And where it exists in sufficient doses, racism can impair social cohesion.

It is the dimension of power, here, that is worth remembering. Racism is troubling because it may allow a group of citizens to feel empowered to subject others to harassment and intimidation.[24] This is something that goes well beyond the objectionable nature of being stereotyped or 'mis-recognised'. As anyone who has been on the receiving end of racist taunts or insults will attest, it can constitute a wounding civic harm in making one feel like a second-class citizen.

Judging without being racist

We may all recognise that racism constitutes a significant harm, but determining what must count as racism isn't always easy. The notion of cultural racism complicates things. Admittedly, what sociologists call cultural racism could be more helpfully labelled as cultural intolerance or cultural bigotry. For if racism can assume a cultural as well as a biological form, this appears to imply that all cultural identities must be entitled to equal respect and recognition. If this is so, there is a danger that multiculturalism's demand for recognition collapses into a form of cultural relativism. But, clearly, there must be limits to what we should recognise as a cultural identity worthy of our respect and endorsement. If not, a community would find it impossible to object to some cultural practices, including those that run counter to fundamental liberal democratic values. Consider, for example, the case of a member of an immigrant community who argues that the practice of polygynist marriage is necessary for the maintenance of their religious or ethnic culture. We could plausibly foresee this citizen contending that a refusal to endorse their practices involves either mis-recognition or non-recognition. Would objecting to such a cultural practice amount to an expression of 'cultural racism'?

This problem is far from hypothetical, as confirmed by ongoing debates about the acceptability of sharia or

Islamic law. Groups such as the Australian Federation of Islamic Councils (AFIC) have argued in favour of formally accommodating aspects of sharia within a system of 'legal pluralism'. According to AFIC, since Islamic law is part of a Muslim's culture, denying its recognition involves an injustice that goes against 'modern standards of citizenship and rights' and 'any profession of multiculturalism'.[25] This example highlights the problem with regarding racism as something based on ideas of cultural incompatibility. For most Australians, sharia evokes an image of a repressive, pre-modern legal system. Many will think of public canings or stonings as punishment for theft or adultery – forms of legal punishment that exist in some countries governed by sharia. Many would be inclined not to countenance its formal accommodation in a secular liberal democratic society (or, for that matter, the formal accommodation of other traditional religious legal codes such as Jewish halacha law or the canon law of the Roman Catholic Church). On the definition of racism outlined above, it is open to question whether this opposition should be categorised as manifesting a form of cultural racism, even if it is motivated by unimpeachably liberal reasons.

Does multiculturalism involve, then, a form of cultural permissiveness?[26] Some interpret a multicultural approach to identity to mean that we must acknowledge all cultures as being of equal value, even if they are antagonistic to liberal values such as individual liberty and equality of the sexes. Properly understood, multi-culturalism doesn't sanction a form of relativism. In practice, as I've shown, multicultural policy in Australia has been circumscribed by the civic values of liberal democracy. Culture isn't a blanket excuse. Any right to express one's cultural identity has been accompanied by a responsibility to adhere to the rule of law and parliamentary democracy, and to respect individual liberty and equality in its various forms.[27] Yet perhaps more needs to be said about why, philosophically, this must also the case.

The key lies in understanding what cultural recognition actually requires. This is the central organising principle of multiculturalism. As I explained in Chapter 2, its civic aspiration concerns the idea of equal recognition: the idea that society should recognise not only the distinctive identity of an individual, but also their cultural group identity. At the most general level, though, equal recognition doesn't mean that cultural practices must be immune from judgement. In a liberal democracy that protects individual liberty and is governed by equality, there are some cases where we must decline to endorse some forms of diversity. What multiculturalism requires – this is the nuance that isn't always understood – is that any refusal is done in the right way. Namely, it must be done with what Taylor calls a 'presumption' that we owe equal respect to all cultures; that all cultures may have something important to say to all human beings.[28] That we are talking only about a presumption is the key point: it is something that may be rebutted. Multiculturalism doesn't ask for an automatic judgement of equal value and worth.[29]

Let's tie this back to the case of judging a cultural identity to be incompatible with a broader Australian national culture. Multiculturalism doesn't mean closing down debate or abrogating free speech on matters of culture. It doesn't legislate that judgements of cultural incompatibility are acts of cultural racism. It simply demands that citizens only arrive at such judgements through a process of public dialogue. It demands a certain political culture.[30]

This has some implications for the nature of free speech and expression, to be sure. While citizens should be free to make a judgement about cultural identities or practices when called upon to do so, they shouldn't be free to engage in forms of racial vilification. No freedom of speech or expression exists without moral or legal limits. In the Australian case, the Commonwealth *Racial Discrimination Act* makes it unlawful for a person to 'offend, insult, humiliate or intimidate another person or a group of people' on the grounds of 'race, colour or national or ethnic origin'. These provisions, under Section 18C of the Act, were relied upon by Aboriginal plaintiffs in a controversial case involving newspaper columnist Andrew Bolt, who was alleged to have engaged in racist and unlawful speech in writing that 'fair-skinned'

Aboriginal people were motivated to identify as Aboriginals in order to advance their professional careers (in September 2011, the Federal Court found that Bolt had indeed breached the *Racial Discrimination Act*). A dejected but unrepentant Bolt maintained after his trial that the Act is evidence of how multiculturalism means that 'you ... may lose your right to speak', if 'your adjectives are too sharp, your wit too pointed, your views too blunt, your observations not quite to the point, your teasing too ticklish and your facts not in every case exactly correct'.[31]

This isn't actually true. There are, in fact, provisions in the Act which provide a free speech exemption. Provided that someone engages in a debate that is in the public interest, and does so in good faith, they cannot be deemed to have breached anti-discrimination law – even if their speech causes offence to people on the grounds of race or ethnicity. In the case of Bolt, the Court found that no such good faith was shown: the articles in question contained 'errors of fact, distortions of the truth and inflammatory and provocative language'.[32] The episode should remind us that if we are to take values of equality and human dignity seriously in a multicultural society, we must be prepared to debate issues of culture and identity according to a certain *ethos* of mutual respect.

This point about a multicultural ethos is about more than just avoiding racial vilification. Where it is an exercise in liberal nation-building, multiculturalism requires nations to be open to revising a public understanding of their collective identity; it isn't confined to requiring that immigrants learn the ways of the majority or the dominant culture. Cultural recognition, in other words, isn't a one-way act of a mainstream adjudicating on a minority's request for some differentiated treatment. It involves a two-way process of interpreting and re-interpreting a national identity. There may be occasions when some cultural practices are ruled incompatible with a broader national culture, as may be the case with sharia. But the demand of multiculturalism is that a community reflect upon its own way of life as well as upon a minority culture when it evaluates an identity or practice.[33] A public dialogue of this sort involves outcomes that aren't final but part of an ongoing process of democratic discussion. When, say, a community declines to give formal recognition to a cultural identity or practice, there may be an eventual revisiting of the issue at a later time. What may prove incompatible with the broader civic culture today may not be so in a decade or two's time.

Thus, on matters such as sharia law, it doesn't suffice merely to make a summary declaration that 'This is how we do things here'. Any debate should at least reflect on why it is that Australia can accommodate cultural, religious and ethnic pluralism, but not pluralism of the legal form.[34] The case of sharia should be an occasion to consider precisely why it is that an Australian society should adhere to a unitary legal system with 'one law for all'.

There are, I believe, good reasons for rejecting any legal pluralism that appeals to a multicultural justification – whether that concerns sharia or halacha or canon law.[35] Establishing multiple legal jurisdictions can empower a community to abuse the individual rights of its members. Any liberal multiculturalism mustn't restrict the ability of individuals in a group (particularly women) to question, revise or abandon traditional roles and practices. Multicultural citizens should be free to reject some practices as incompatible with a broader civic culture without lapsing into a form of 'cultural racism' – provided the judgement is arrived at through a process of collective dialogue or deliberation.[36]

What's a national identity and culture?

So far, I have argued that any claim for cultural recognition must be judged against a broader civic culture. But what constitutes this culture? We might ask whether asserting a civic culture simply ends up confirming that minorities must conform to a dominant white or Anglo-Celtic culture.

Many fail to distinguish between the civic character of national culture and its ethnic, lifestyle dimensions. I reflect, for example, on an exchange I had in late 2009 with *Crikey* writer and satirist Guy Rundle about the content of an Australian national culture. For Rundle, being an Australian came down to a question of lifestyle: in his case, nothing was more Australian than the authenticity of plunging into the water on a surf beach, a game of French cricket, the sharp taste of VB, Cold Chisel on the juke box, glimpsing girls in Rip Curl tops, and Sunnyboy ice-blocks. If this self-described Anglo-Celtic lifestyle should exclude people of immigrant minority backgrounds, according to Rundle, then that is 'tough'.[37] Of course, the likes of Rundle shouldn't assume that those of ethnic minority background can only ever be exotic ethnics. That an Asian-Australian, for example, could be familiar with the beach, the cricket or Australian rock music is, for Rundle, evidently unthinkable. His implied suggestion was that you couldn't really be authentically Australian, or have anything of value to contribute to a national conversation, unless you could draw upon some transcendental experience of sucking on Sunnyboys at the beach, and sipping VB while perving on chicks in skimpy tops. It is like suggesting that one can only possess an Australian spirit if one crushes some eucalyptus leaves and inhales.[38]

We can distinguish between two senses in which we discuss national culture. To use the distinction adopted by political philosopher David Miller, there is first a 'public culture', which provides guidance on how a community should conduct its life together. This includes not only political values such as a commitment to democracy or the rule of law, but also some social norms or manners (things like whether you are honest in filling out your tax return, how you queue at a bus stop, or the formality with which you address a stranger). A public culture shouldn't be confused with a 'private culture', which covers those beliefs and preferences that are likely to be shared within a family, an ethnic community or a lifestyle enclave.[39] Within a national public culture, there will be room for many different private cultures.

So when we talk about an Australian civic culture, we're referring not to those things people may ordinarily associate with an Australian cultural lifestyle. We are referring instead to things such as an Australian tradition of parliamentary democracy, a belief in a 'fair go' and a certain egalitarianism. And while an Australian civic culture may well encompass some social norms such as taking turns buying 'shouts' or calling someone by their first name even if we're not familiar with them, it isn't accurately defined by a fondness for sport and barbeques, and a love of sand and surf.[40] These things say very little about how Australians conduct our life together. It makes little sense to say that you can only count as an Australian – or a 'true' Australian – if you spend your Saturdays in summer grilling snags, watching the cricket or catching some waves. Many of us may well do this; then again, many of us don't.

To return to the matter of public dialogue about culture, it can't ever be enough to declare that something is incompatible with a private 'Australian' culture – that a practice or identity is incompatible with an Australian way of life we'd associate with sport, meat pies and the beach. It is a different story if something is incompatible with democratic values such as fairness or equality.

It is open to debate, of course, whether the kind of public culture I have put forward will resonate with enough Australians to count as a basis for national unity. We can only hope that Australians take the idea of a civic culture built on democracy, fairness and equality seriously enough, and certainly more seriously than a creed of sun, sand and surf. Otherwise the Australian nation would be nothing more than a lifestyle nation. If this line of argument should upset people like Rundle, well, tough.

A more serious question concerns whether any civic culture can be separated from an Anglo-Celtic 'holding' culture. Some scholars of Australian citizenship and national identity contend that it cannot, saying that it is the Anglo-Celtic core of Australianness that provides the foundation for the national identity, providing a historical coherence that otherwise isn't there. The best way to avoid social fragmentation, according to this view, is to ensure that immigrants from a diverse ethnic mix can be integrated into the Anglo-Celtic identity consistent with an 'old Australia'.[41]

But if there is to be a unifying culture, it's important not to invoke an Australian civic culture as a euphemism for an Anglo-Celtic ethnic culture. The reason is simple: how exactly can those with backgrounds other than Anglo-Celtic truly feel Australian if they are to be reminded that their place in the national story lies only at the periphery? This is one problem that some advocates of the Anglo-Celtic 'holding' culture argument don't address convincingly.

A national public culture, defined as a civic rather than an Anglo-Celtic culture, remains the most viable basis for a common identity. It provides a set of common institutions and shared values and norms, but it isn't about ethnicity, lifestyle or ancestral origin. As applied to Australia, a national public culture means there should be no expectation that immigrants conform to an Anglo-Celtic ethnic culture, even if many may well end up doing so. What ultimately matters is that everyone is prepared to sign up to an Australian democratic culture. As for Anglo-Celtic Australians, any 'ownership' of the national culture should be qualified – and not only by recognition of Indigenous Australians and their position as the traditional owners of country. Because of cultural diversity, there is no longer a typical way of being Australian, as there may once have been for Nino Culottas to emulate. Where we define national culture predominantly in civic terms, all citizens have the opportunity to contribute to the content of the national identity.

One dimension of an Australian identity that must reflect the contributions of its members is national history. A civic culture can't just be about values – it would otherwise amount to 'a cold and cerebral formula'.[42] It must also contain some historical content that differentiates an Australian civic culture from that of any other liberal polity. In the Australian case, our civic culture is supported by a certain experience, incorporating the colonial experience of self-government, Federation and democratic innovation (for instance, we are one of the oldest democracies in the world, and were among the first nations to allow women to vote). And it also incorporates foundational aspects of national history, such as the Anzac legend. It is only through the flesh of such things that a civic culture comes to take on a distinctive national character.

An obvious challenge with all this is to articulate a civic culture or national public culture that isn't defined by Anglo-Celtic Australian nationhood. The task here isn't to repudiate a national history and start afresh. Rather, it is to draw upon the *best of* any historical tradition, so as to ensure it is as inclusive as possible. This is one way, for example, to deal with the challenge of reconciling Anzac Day remembrance with a multicultural Australia. While many would regard Anzac Day as one of the most important days of the Australian calendar, it remains unclear for many without an ancestral connection to Gallipoli or other Australian war experiences how they should relate to it. This is presumably one reason why a 2010 report commissioned by the Commonwealth Department of Veterans' Affairs in preparation for the centenary commemoration of Anzac Day observed that 'commemorating our military history in a multicultural society is something of a doubled-edged sword'. While the centenary of Anzac Day could 'provide some opportunity for creating a greater sense of unity, it is also recognised as a potential area of divisiveness'.[43]

The wording of this concern perhaps isn't quite right, insofar as it suggests there are Australians of immigrant background who take offence at Anzac Day commemorations. There is no evidence of that. It isn't so much that Anzac Day might be divisive as that the day mightn't necessarily resonate in the same way for all Australians. Indeed, the day can loom as one of atavistic national commemoration. With its popular resurgence during the past decade or so, Anzac Day has become increasingly marked by a cultural or militaristic celebration of Australianness – as revealed by ubiquitous comments about the sacrifice of heroic Anzacs in defending an 'Australian way of life', which is often in the public mind associated with a distinctive national lifestyle.[44] Anzac Day is also frequently reduced to its ancestral dimensions – a day for Australians to remember the experiences of their forebears, whether it is those who fought in Gallipoli or on the Western Front, or on the Kokoda trail, or in more recent military engagements. Either way, when questions about how a multicultural Australia fits in with Anzac Day are raised, the public response isn't always reassuring. When in March 2012 the *Herald Sun* newspaper reported on its front page that the Commonwealth government had been 'warned' that 'celebrating the centenary of Anzac Day could provoke division in multicultural Australia', it sparked inevitable anger and outrage about unnecessary political correctness.[45]

If we adopt an ethnic or genealogical understanding of the nation, it is hard to see how more recent arrivals to Australia can find meaning in Anzac Day. Remembrance in that case is about the 'crimson thread of kinship'. But where we take a civic understanding of the nation, a different approach is possible. Without denying the power that Anzac Day has for many Australians with forebears who served their country, we can say that the commemoration of Anzac Day is an occasion for all Australians to remember the sacrifices of past citizens. It should be a day that reminds us of the sacrifices that the responsibilities of citizenship may demand of us *in extremis*, without lapsing into a crude celebration of militarism and war.

In any case, multicultural realities may require a more challenging form of national reflection upon Anzac Day. While the reportage of Ellis Ashmead-Bartlett and Charles Bean may have celebrated the virile virtues of Anzac soldiers, an affirmation of the strength of an Australian 'race', even the Anzac tradition involves a certain pluralism. We often forget that General John Monash was the son of Jews from Germany. There are also unlikely dashes of an Asian flavour elsewhere. To give but a few examples, one of the more celebrated soldiers in Gallipoli and France during the First World War was a sniper by the name of Billy Sing, an Australian born to a Chinese father and an English mother. For many years, the Anzac Day march in Perth featured the popular veteran Jack Wong Sue, a Chinese-Australian who was part of an Allied commando unit in the Second World War, Z Special Unit, which operated behind Japanese lines in Borneo. Historian Kate Bagnall has recently uncovered the story of one mixed Anglo-Chinese Australian family, the Sams of West Wyalong in New South Wales, whose five sons enlisted for service in the First World War.[46]

It is important to view the Anzac tradition not only as a civic touchstone of the Australian experience but also one that reflects – if only in fragments – Australia's pluralism. I have often reflected on this as someone who, for many years, struggled to relate to Anzac Day. As a teenager, I often found myself at a loss when others spoke about the sacrifice made by 'our forebears', knowing that my own grandfathers and great-grandfathers in China and Laos would probably not even have known that Australia existed. Had I been aware of the contributions of Anglo-Chinese diggers such as Sing or Sue or the Sam brothers, I suspect I might have had a slightly different response to Anzac, all those years ago.

From ethnic politics to ethnics in politics

The challenge doesn't end with national history. While there is much truth to the Orwellian dictum that 'He who controls the past controls the future', the present obviously counts for a lot as well. How our cultural diversity is reflected in contemporary Australian society matters.

Let's begin with the realm of the state, by which I mean our institutions of government. With the advent of multicultural policy, governments have obviously supported the expression of cultural diversity through the funding of ethnic community organisations and activities. In a very practical sense, the policy of multiculturalism has also ensured that government conducts its affairs in a way that is responsive to cultural diversity. The evolution of multiculturalism from the Whitlam government to the Fraser governments to the Hawke–Keating governments saw the eventual emergence of the principle of access and equity. In its various successive forms, this has since guided Commonwealth and most state and territory governments in their delivery of services. Multiculturalism has meant that governments no longer deliver public services in a uniform fashion, blind to the needs of a diverse population.

However, the delivery of public services isn't the only thing that matters for multiculturalism. Some would say that any recognition of diversity must go much deeper –

that is, to the fundamental structures of the state itself. Now that Australian society is multicultural, isn't it time that the Australian nation-state be radically reconstituted as multicultural? According to historian Alastair Davidson, liberal multicultural policies may do as much to stifle diversity as to allow it to flourish. In his view, official multiculturalism may have offered immigrants a right to cultural diversity, but this right has never extended to being able to criticise the existing political and legal structures in Australia. A form of Anglo-Celtic community still defines the theory and practice of government. The continuing consensus about the superiority of the common law and Westminster-style parliamentary democracy ends up 'silencing the migrant voice':

> It is not flippant to say that a multicultural Australia
> incorporated *souvlaki* and dragon dances, but not the
> legal, political and ethical voices of its myriad NESB
> newcomers. Indeed, on the latter issues the 1995
> position was little different from that expressed
> when the first postwar migrants arrived. They had
> nothing to teach a population which was heir to 600
> years of British legal and political traditions about
> how best to arrange such matters to empower a
> multi-ethnic citizenry.[47]

For critics such as Davidson, what is required is an open

negotiation of the fundamental character of Australian democracy. Australians must be willing to consider arguments that rely upon sources other than English-speaking democratic authority. For example, Italian immigrants should be able to appeal to Italian democratic norms as citizens in Australia – and we should be willing to adopt Italian democratic wisdom. A more thoroughgoing multiculturalism wouldn't close off the prospect of transforming an Australian democratic tradition. It would incorporate the different perspectives of immigrants, even those that don't sit comfortably with representative, parliamentary democracy.

The problem with this argument should be clear. Stability and legitimacy in a political state would be elusive if we subject our public institutions and civic culture to an open slather contest of this sort. As I've argued, any dialogue concerning cultural diversity requires some common ground. There is perhaps one basic misreading involved in the radical critique of liberal multiculturalism. It suggests that any criticism of political and legal structures in Australia must require a complete reconstitution of our public institutions. This, in turn, is based on the dubious assumption that accepting an Australian civic culture, even one defined in terms of parliamentary democracy and the rule of law, amounts to acquiescing to a disguised nationalism with racist qualities.

Still, there is some truth to the criticism that multiculturalism could be better reflected within an existing

Australian civic culture. We could start with our representative political institutions. While parliaments shouldn't necessarily mirror the composition of society, Australians of non-English-speaking background remain somewhat under-represented.[48] For example, of the current 226 Commonwealth parliamentarians, which includes all members of the House of Representatives and the Senate, 12.4 per cent were born overseas, with 3.9 per cent born in a non-English-speaking country. To give some perspective of how this compares to Australian society, Australian Bureau of Statistics data from 2010 indicates that almost 27 per cent of the Australian population was born overseas, with 19 per cent born in countries other than the United Kingdom and New Zealand.[49] Those parliamentarians with a non-English-speaking background are, moreover, overwhelmingly European in background. There are very few from a non-European background. Of the current cohort of federal MPs and senators, there are only three who would fit that description (Senators Penny Wong and Lisa Singh, and Member for Hasluck Ken Wyatt) – a grand total of 1.3 per cent of total federal parliamentarians. The Malaysian-born Finance Minister Penny Wong is the only current parliamentarian born in a country in Asia, while Wyatt is the only current Indigenous parliamentarian.

There are many reasons that account for such under-representation. The organisation of the Australian electoral system in the form of single-member seats is one factor. Were we to have another system in place, for instance a mixed-member proportional system, it is conceivable that a higher proportion of minorities would be represented in parliament. According to Jupp, who conducted an audit of how well Australian democracy serves immigrant Australians, the failure of legislatures to contain diversity is largely due to the political parties. In parliamentary preselections, 'safe seats go to the Australian-born' (it is interesting that the safest Labor seats also tend to be the most ethnically diverse). In many cases, 'where an "ethnic" candidate seems likely to secure preselection for a winnable seat there has been friction and dispute'.[50] Indeed, where immigrant ethnic minority communities have sought to participate in party politics by joining local party branches in an organised fashion, they have been depicted as engaging in 'ethnic branch-stacking'. When done by 'ethnic' politicians, what may otherwise be regarded as recruitment has more often than not been condemned as a form of clientelist politics that has no place in Australian democracy.[51]

Perhaps for a more banal reason, under-representation may simply reflect an inevitable lag between diversity in society and the achievement of diversity within parliament. That there are so few Australian parliamentarians of non-European descent may simply reflect the fact that immigrants from Asia, the Middle East and Africa have been relatively recent arrivals. There is some support for this view, given that there were very few members of parliament of Italian or Greek descent until the past decade or so. Even so, the election of politicians of non-European background shouldn't be taken for granted. The cost of some groups in our society not enjoying a sense of representation in our elected parliaments can potentially be high.

With this in mind, it is worth noting the very small numbers of Asian-Australians in Australian parliaments, particularly at the federal level.[52] There have only been a handful of state parliamentarians of Asian background, though there have been a number of prominent Chinese-Australian lord mayors, including the current Lord Mayor of Darwin, Katrina Fong Lim.[53] There has similarly been only a very small number of politicians from Middle Eastern backgrounds elected to parliament at state and federal levels (with some notable exceptions). Australian political parties could do a better job of ensuring that their parliamentary candidates, particularly at the federal level, reflect more accurately the modern face of Australian society.

The response needn't involve the imposition of quotas or affirmative action, but it must begin with a change in attitude. Sadly, it remains a somewhat common view among political party powerbrokers that the Australian electorate may not necessarily be 'ready' for more ethnic minority representatives. For example, I remember one former senior Labor party adviser in New South Wales, himself with some non-English-speaking heritage, once saying to me that if I ever entertained the idea of running for parliament I'd have to change my long 'ethnic' surname.

Problems of under-representation in public institutions aren't confined to parliaments but are also present in the Australian public service (APS). In 2011 a mere 5.1 per cent of APS employees identified themselves as being from a non-English-speaking background. This number has barely changed from 4.5 per cent in 2002.[54] In some central federal government departments, such as the Department of the Prime Minister and Cabinet, the figure is a paltry 2.6 per cent. Faring even worse is the Department of Defence, where only 1.7 per cent of civilian APS employees are from a non-English-speaking background.[55]

The situation is similar in the Australian Defence Force (ADF). According to the 2007 Defence census, 94 per cent of permanent members of the ADF were born in either Australia, the UK, Ireland or New Zealand – with only 1 per cent of permanent members born in Asia.[56] Arguably, the case of Defence is exacerbated by the presence of subcultures in the ADF which have been hostile towards cultural diversity (and women). This has been evident in periodic episodes involving racist behavior by ADF personnel – for instance, involving soldiers' participation in online forums expressing shocking hostility towards immigrants and Muslims.[57] The problem is openly recognised by military brass. In February 2012, the Chief of Army, Lieutenant General David Morrison, acknowledged in a speech that the Army's culture 'has tended to exclude women and some ethnic groups who are under-represented in our ranks'.[58] While it may not seem obvious to link the question of representation of minorities in the defence forces with the public service more generally, there is a common equation: in both cases we are talking about central institutions of the state which have clearly struggled in dealing with diversity.

Discrimination in the workplace and the media

There remains the broader realm of Australian society – among other things, the workplace and the media. As with government institutions, the results are mixed. Yet in many ways how multiculturalism fares in these areas is of greater importance than how it fares in government. After all, the workplace and media touch upon the everyday lives of most Australians.[59]

This is most true of the workplace. The ability of those from minority, immigrant backgrounds to participate in the labour market and obtain secure employment is crucial to the success of a multicultural society. For the most part, immigrants have generally been well integrated into the Australian economy. As outlined in Chapter 1, immigrants helped to meet the demand for labour during a postwar period of reconstruction. With the structural shift to a more internationalised and service-based economy, there has been a deliberate shift towards skilled immigration (marked by the introduction of a 'points test' in 1979). During the past 15 years or so, the skilled immigrant stream has also been extended by the introduction of temporary skilled worker schemes (such as the '457' skilled visa scheme). To give some indication of the orientation of the Australian immigration intake, the federal government has recently affirmed its commitment to selecting 'the best and brightest skilled migrants by emphasising high level qualifications', along with better English levels and 'extensive skilled work experience'.[60] The combination of these factors – a high level of demand for labour in the postwar period and high selectivity since the late 1970s – has ensured that newly arrived immigrants have tended to find employment readily. This is true of the vast majority of skilled immigrants today. Recently arrived skilled immigrants have an unemployment rate well below the national average, and a participation rate of 95 per cent (compared to the national average of 65 per cent).[61]

Despite this, there remains some degree of ethnic hierarchy in the labour market. The situation isn't as pronounced as it may have been in the past. The economy of the postwar decades was organised on the basis that immigrants, particularly those from non-English-speaking backgrounds, would occupy the lower rungs of the labour force; immigrants weren't arriving to compete for jobs, but rather to do jobs that ensured Australians could enjoy higher living standards. But, even in an era of skilled immigration, those from non-English-speaking backgrounds still appear to suffer from some structural disadvantage in the labour market.[62] The average employment outcomes for those with tertiary educational qualifications who are of non-European origin are significantly poorer than for those who are Australian-born or UK-born. This can be interpreted as evidence that 'cultural stereotyping, prejudice and discrimination may be affecting a significant portion of the workforce'.[63]

The truth is the cause of any structural disadvantage mightn't be easy to identify. Where there is unfair workplace or employment discrimination, it frequently concerns the way that employers evaluate things such as 'soft skills'. Yet these are often the factors that have the most influence on decisions within the workplace. When it comes to getting a job or landing a promotion, an employer's judgement about whether there is a good 'cultural fit' is just as important as more objective factors such as qualifications or language proficiency. There is also the issue of formal recognition of overseas qualifications. Stories about foreign-trained doctors, engineers and teachers driving taxis in Sydney and Melbourne because Australian professional bodies don't recognise their qualifications are legion.

Discrimination of a more blatant form also exists. One widely reported study by economists Alison Booth,

Andrew Leigh and Elena Varganova found substantial discrimination in hiring by Australian employers. They sent over 4000 fake job applications for entry-level waiting, data entry, customer service and sales jobs, all containing the same qualifications but with different names. The results may surprise some – not so much because they revealed that having an Anglo-Saxon name meant one was more likely to garner an employer's interest, but because of the extent to which this was so. For applicants with Anglo-Saxon names, there was a 35 per cent chance of getting asked in for an interview. This was true for only 32 per cent of those with Italian names, 26 per cent with Indigenous names, 22 per cent with Middle Eastern names and just 21 per cent with Chinese names. In order to get as many interviews as an applicant with an Anglo-Saxon name, someone with a Chinese name would have to submit 68 per cent more applications; those with a Middle Eastern name would need 64 per cent more; those with an Indigenous name 35 per cent more; and those with an Italian name 12 per cent more.[64] These aren't the kind of results a multicultural society would accept as satisfactory. They clearly point to significant racial and ethnic discrimination among Australian employers. Rectifying this isn't easy. We already have anti-discrimination laws in place. But changing people's attitudes takes time. It is a reminder that we shouldn't be complacent about prejudice and discrimination.

If racism and discrimination in the workplace have the potential to incur the greatest practical cost for most people, racism and discrimination in the media have the potential for the highest symbolic cost. The importance of how diversity is represented in media shouldn't be underestimated. The way a national community understands its collective identity will be reflected in its media, in particular television. Unfortunately, the Australian media doesn't do as well as it should. For supporters of multiculturalism, this has been a perennial bugbear: programs on television have never been representative of cultural diversity as it exists in Australian cities and suburbs. Two or three decades ago, ethnic and cultural homogeneity in Australian television may have been understandable; this seems less forgivable today.

Things aren't this way because of a want of criticism. Prominent actors of minority cultural backgrounds have increasingly drawn attention to the enduring white complexion of Australian television. In the words of Firass Dirani, the lead actor in the highly successful drama *Underbelly: The Golden Mile*, it was time for commercial television to dump its de facto 'White Australia' policy. As Dirani put it, while modern Australia means that 'when you walk down Sydney streets you see so many different cultures and so many different people', television writers and producers fail to 'create roles for people from a broad range of cultural backgrounds'.[65] If there is something deflating about Dirani's comments, it is that they don't seem altogether different from the remarks made by Al Grassby in 1973 about the failure of television screens to 'reflect anything like the variety of migrant groups encountered through our city streets'. As Grassby put it: 'The image we manage to convey of ourselves still seems to range from the bushwalker to the sportsman to the slick businessman. Where is the Maltese process worker, the Finnish carpenter, the Italian concrete layer, the Yugoslav miner or ... the Indian scientist?'[66]

A revealing example is that of *Neighbours*, Australia's longest-running soap drama. The program has been on air since 1985, but there hasn't yet been a character of Asian background who has lasted much more than a year in the program. To be fair, this may be about to change. Amid much fanfare in February 2012, the producers of *Neighbours* introduced an Indian family to Ramsay Street: the Kapoors. Yet past experience suggests we shouldn't be too optimistic about how long they might remain. In 2005, the first attempt by producers to write in some regular Asian cast members, the Lims, saw the family last a pathetic six weeks before disappearing from Erinsborough. The much publicised introduction of the character Sunny Lee, a Korean exchange student, into the *Neighbours* cast of 2008 was also rather shortlived, though what is perhaps most notable about Sunny was her transient status as an exchange student (clearly, the idea of a permanent Asian presence in the world of Erinsborough is unthinkable). This is to say nothing of the comical attempts by *Neighbours* writers to integrate characters of other ethnic background into their narrative arc. One of the few minority families to grace Ramsay Street, the Cammenitis, who lasted in the program from 2003 to 2008, would reprise stereotypes of Italian Mafiosa (the father Rocco was a local Mafioso) and of 'feisty' and 'passionate' Italian females (as sisters Carmella, Rosetta and Sienna would be described in Channel Ten publicity).

Writer Daniel Burt has remarked that if television is indeed something of a mirror for society, Australian television is 'one of those square metal sheets that they put above the sink in public toilets ... you might recognise the shape but the detail is distorted and looking at it can make you feel dirty'.[67] The usual excuses of producers and television writers – that inserting 'ethnic' characters amounts to mere tokenism and fails to appeal audiences – seem disingenuous. It is arguably no accident that recent ratings successes such as *Australian Idol* and *MasterChef* have been notable for embracing the authentic diversity of Australian society rather than considering it as a handicap to popularity. How telling it is that after more than 25 years, *Neighbours* has produced no equivalent of a Guy Sebastian or a Poh Ling Yeow – only Kylie Minogues and Delta Goodrems.

The overwhelming absence of diversity on television screens isn't the only problem. When ethnic and cultural minorities do appear in fictional dramas, they often appear in dubious contexts – as illustrated by the Mafia example of Rocco Cammeniti and more recently by *Underbelly*, in which the alleged Kings Cross organised crime figure John Ibrahim was portrayed by Dirani. The problem also extends to how ethnic and cultural minorities are depicted in factual and current affairs programming.

Popular programs such as *Today Tonight* and *A Current Affair* frequently resort to provocative misrepresentations. One episode of *Today Tonight* in October 2011 falsely portrayed asylum seekers and refugees as living in luxurious accommodation, and as the beneficiaries of generous welfare benefits funded by Australian taxpayers. To cite the words of host Kylie Gillies, the story was an 'investigation into how the government is putting out the welcome mat for refugees', citing the payment of $400 a week in benefits to refugees (actual payments were significantly lower) and showing photographs of supposed tourist excursions by refugees while in detention (they were photographs of refugees taken after they were released from detention).[68]

Another egregious example is an episode of *A Current Affair* from 2007, which purported to offer an exclusive report of going 'behind enemy lines' in Egypt on a 'secret mission' to help Samantha Cambridge recover her five-year-old daughter Levana, who had been 'kidnapped' by Cambridge's estranged Egyptian husband. In the program's own colourful language, it was a story about a little girl who had been 'abducted for being Australian' by 'extremist Muslims' who were holding her hostage.

No effort was made by the program to substantiate any of the claims. Australia was never, of course, at war with Egypt in 2007; there is no evidence for either Levana abducted for 'being Australian' or that 'extremist' Islamism had anything to do with the episode.

More recently, *A Current Affair* led an episode in April 2012 with a story titled 'Asian bride invasion', the suggestion being that an alleged 'influx' of mail-order brides was beginning to place strains on Australia's immigration system.[69] A few weeks later in May 2012, rival *Today Tonight* responded by sending Pauline Hanson to south-east Asia 'undercover' to expose a 'sinister black market passport trade' supposedly threatening Australian national security. In both cases, all that was on display was tabloid reprisal of old fears about Australia being invaded by yellow hordes from Asia.[70]

There is one institution that offsets, however partially, the monocultural character and content of mainstream Australian media. The Special Broadcasting Service (SBS) has, since its establishment in 1980, been an institutional pillar of Australian multiculturalism. It is one of the key expressions of how Australia regards itself as a nation of cultural diversity. The SBS Charter states that the principal function of SBS is 'to provide multilingual and multicultural radio and television services that inform, educate and entertain all Australians, and, in doing so, reflect Australia's multicultural society'.[71] With this mission, SBS is truly unique: even in Canada, the other notable country that embraces an official multiculturalism, there is no equivalent. And, for the past three decades, it has fulfilled its purpose with considerable success, albeit while incurring periodic criticism. From its inception, SBS has been dismissed as either a divisive or outdated exercise in 'ethnic' media. Others, meanwhile, have lambasted the broadcaster for becoming too commercialised and 'mainstream', at the expense of multicultural communities. Yet by virtue of its ongoing presence in the national media, SBS has guaranteed that diversity is represented in what we hear on radio and see on television. Even for those who never listen to or watch SBS, the very presence of it on the free-to-air spectrum and on the radio waves is a constant reminder that Australia is a multicultural society.[72]

It has been through its television programming that SBS has had its most profound impact. SBS Radio tends to serve the needs of newly arrived immigrant communities and has historically been closely associated with an ethno-specific approach to multiculturalism. The more prominent division of SBS Television has a much wider reach (even if its audience share remains small compared with the commercial networks and also the ABC). SBS Television programming has helped to encourage a more pluralistic world view among Australians – one that 'entails openness towards different cultures and peoples' and 'helps overcome intolerance and enhances intercultural understanding'.[73]

Such an outward-looking perspective is nurtured by, among other things, SBS's world news service and its regular broadcasting of international films. The broadcaster has also ensured there has been factual programming on free-to-air television that has sought to reflect explicitly on the impact of immigration and debates about diversity. Recent notable examples include *Go Back To Where You Came From* (dealing with the issue of asylum and boat people) and *Once Upon a Time in Cabramatta* (dealing with the experience of the Vietnamese community in Cabramatta). More generally, SBS's news reporting and current affairs programs such as *Insight* consistently cover Australian and international issues with a multicultural awareness that its commercial and ABC counterparts lack. The fact that SBS news presenters have always been of ethnic minority backgrounds shouldn't be dismissed as a trivial detail: it matters that a young Australian child from an immigrant background can see someone other than the Peter Overtons, Jo Halls or Chris Baths presenting the evening news.

But it is in another respect that SBS makes its most profound contribution to ensuring an unapologetic and forthright representation of cultural diversity on national television. Through innovative dramas such as *East West 101* and *The Circuit*, SBS helps convey a dose of 'popular multiculturalism' by not treating multicultural diversity as a special theme but rather validating it 'as an increasingly ordinary, taken-for-granted feature of everyday life'.[74] What is striking in such programming is not only the full spectrum of colour in its cast – as dramatic a contrast to *Neighbours* and *Packed to the Rafters* as one could imagine – but that the diversity of the cast isn't portrayed as exotic. This captures powerfully the manner in which SBS today can best fulfil its charter. At the most fundamental level, there are two kinds of multiculturalism. There can be a 'protective' one, which aims to preserve the integrity of cultural identities from change. And there can be a 'pluralistic' multiculturalism, which is centred on expanding the range of options available to all members of the community, including members of a majority group.[75] In making diversity banal and part of the everyday background in which Australians live their lives, SBS television helps to secure the conditions of a pluralistic multiculturalism.

It is hard to imagine Australian multiculturalism without SBS, even if there are perennial debates about its relevance and about merging it with the ABC. We shouldn't forget the distinctive contribution that a multicultural broadcaster makes to Australian sensibilities about diversity. The persistence of racism in Australian society at a number of levels and the poor representation of minority faces and voices in the national media mean that SBS remains integral to the project of multiculturalism. Given that legislation can only go so far in changing attitudes, the power of the media to shape collective identities is one of the most important instruments available for achieving a more open, understanding and deliberative citizenry. At the same time, the real challenge for Australian society is to ensure that SBS isn't the only public institution that is authentically multicultural. It remains important to ensure that all areas of the nation's life – whether that is in government, the workplace or the media – are genuinely open to the contributions of all Australians. Of course, there's no simple fix available. It is a reminder that multiculturalism, for all that has been done in its name, continues to embody an aspiration.

4

A bigger Australia

Prime ministers in Australia, unlike presidents in the US, don't have inaugurations at which they declare their program for government. But this doesn't mean they don't use their first speeches to signal how they will govern. In July 2010, two weeks after replacing Kevin Rudd as Prime Minister, Julia Gillard delivered her first significant policy speech to an audience at the Lowy Institute in Sydney. There was a symmetry to the occasion: here was Gillard, Australia's first overseas-born Prime Minister since Billy Hughes, speaking at a think tank founded by one of Australia's most distinguished immigrants, billionaire Frank Lowy (who was also a Jewish refugee from central Europe).

Yet what she actually said seemed to jar with the nation-building history of Australia's immigration experience. There was a reiteration that she didn't endorse her predecessor's vision of a 'big Australia' with a population of 36 million by 2050. According to Gillard, 'a national leader must recognise when a government needs to take a breath, slow down, weigh the evidence and make the right, considered judgements for our people'. On that basis, 'I support sustainable population growth and reject the idea that Australia should hurtle down the track towards a big population'.[1] Gillard then proceeded to outline Labor's new asylum seeker policy, based on the establishment of a regional processing centre for boat arrivals in East Timor. The next day, she travelled to Darwin. Television news that evening was dominated by images of her aboard a naval patrol boat, one of the vessels used by the Navy to intercept unauthorised boats in Australian waters. Standing beside her on the patrol boat was David Bradbury, the member for the western Sydney electorate of Lindsay.

The asylum seeker issue, specifically the arrival of boats, would feature prominently in the election campaign of 2010. Tony Abbott adopted 'Stop the boats' as his signature slogan; Labor would respond with earnest pledges to stop people smugglers. But what was striking in Gillard's presentation of the issue at the Lowy Institute was the manner in which she explicitly tied it to concerns about population growth, particularly among those living in the outer suburbs of western Sydney. In a speech ostensibly concerned with asylum seekers, Gillard would observe that 'people would laugh if you told them population was intended to improve living standards', and that those 'on the front line of our population increase ... know that bigger isn't necessarily better'.[2]

As if to underline her response to such concern, one of Gillard's first moves as Prime Minister was to amend Tony Burke's ministerial title from Minister for Population to Minister for Sustainable Population. For many, the retreat from population growth and immigration, along with a hardened posture on asylum seekers, could be seen as a proxy attack on the conditions for a multi-cultural Australia.

In much of the public imagination, issues concerning multiculturalism, immigration and population are certainly melded into one. Perhaps it is because politicians themselves conflate the issues, as Gillard did in her Lowy Institute speech. But it is important to clarify the relationship between them. The connections that exist between immigration and population are clear enough: population issues in Australia have traditionally concerned settlement and immigration. Precisely where multiculturalism fits into the picture is less clear. Indeed, some would argue that debates about multiculturalism – concerning questions of cultural accommodation, integration and identity – are best conducted when decoupled from debates about immigration and population. This would ensure, the argument runs, that any antagonism towards multicultural policy doesn't undermine broader public support for a non-racially-discriminatory immigration policy, or distort policy-making about Australia's long-term population. Any concerns about population growth should be regarded as primarily a challenge for public policy in infrastructure and planning rather than in multiculturalism.

Quarantining multicultural issues in this fashion is unlikely to be successful. It has always been difficult to divorce concerns about multiculturalism from immigration. Multicultural policy emerged as a response to the cultural pluralism created by successive waves of mass immigration. And where multiculturalism has been criticised or attacked, this has tended to be tied to calls for lower levels of immigration – as in the cases of Blainey and Howard in the 1980s and Hanson in the 1990s. This historical connection is one factor that distinguishes Australian debates from debates in Canada, that other country with an official multiculturalism. In Canada, discussions of multiculturalism have generally encompassed questions about the treatment of indigenous First Nations Canadians. Here, they have remained largely confined to ones about immigrants and their integration into Australian society. Unlike our Canadian counterparts, we seem wary of associating reconciliation and diversity too closely, lest it imply that Indigenous Australians are just another minority cultural group rather than traditional owners of country.

There are also inevitable connections made between multiculturalism and population policy, given the strong cultural inflection in much of the concern about population growth. More often than not, the concern reveals a desire for cultural security, which isn't necessarily sympathetic to cultural diversity and immigration. Population growth is perceived as a threat to a national lifestyle – a traditional Australian way of life. It is seen as a destroyer of a comfortable existence in the suburbs, with large, green backyards in which children could play cricket, climb trees and roam 'free range'.[3] At the same time, the cultural consequences of population growth may run in the other direction. There is the possibility that where population growth occurs too quickly, the capacity to sustain a harmonious and cohesive society may become impaired. A bigger Australia, were it to come into being too rapidly, could be bad news for Australian multiculturalism. In light of ongoing concerns about population growth, the question seems to be which version is more accurate. Must the logic of supporting a multicultural Australia mean also supporting a bigger Australia? Or might it require supporting the opposite?

The economics of a bigger Australia

The notion of an Australian continent populated by many more millions has long excited Australians – even prior to Federation. A big Australia was a matter of national destiny. On the occasion of the 1888 centenary of Arthur Phillip's landing with the First Fleet in Sydney, a correspondent for the *Spectator* of London noted that, 'There is every reasonable probability that in 1988 Australia will be a Federal Republic, peopled by 50 millions of English speaking men ...'.[4] It wasn't until after the First World War and the 1920s that such ambition would reach its peak. Journalist Edwin Brady's label of 'Australia Unlimited' became a popular catchphrase. 'Very early in the country's history', Brady wrote, 'there arose a stereotyped conception of the interior as a dry and waterless desert, composed for the most part of shifting sands, scorched by everlasting suns and swept by constant hot winds'. This was untrue, he argued, suggesting that 'it is doubtful if there are a hundred square miles of true desert within the whole area of the Australian continent'.[5] Australia was a land of abundant land and riches, which needed only capital and labour to blossom. Prime Minister Stanley Bruce, who shared Brady's expansive credo, believed that development was dependent upon 'men, money and markets'. On the question of 'men', between 1920 and 1929 net overseas migration to Australia exceeded 300 000 people, with more than 200 000 Britons enjoying assisted passage financed by the British government. Most British emigrants would be encouraged to go onto the land – part of an imperial bargain in which Australia Unlimited would export wool and wheat, meat and sugar to Britain.[6]

Any such project of national development was interrupted, first by the Great Depression of the 1930s and then by the Second World War. It wasn't until after the war that a concerted policy of boosting Australia's population would be revisited, under the direction of

Arthur Calwell. As noted in Chapter 1, there was a remarkably robust bipartisan commitment to the postwar immigration program. Only in the late 1960s and early 1970s were the first signs of dissent voiced in public debate. This would be led by scientific concern about the rate of global population growth, as exemplified by biologist Paul Ehrlich's bestselling book of 1968 *The Population Bomb*.[7] By the 1990s there were increasing demands for an explicit population policy which would be sensitive to the environmental impact of immigration.[8]

In the view of a 1994 parliamentary inquiry studying Australia's population 'carrying capacity' (chaired by former Science Minister Barry Jones, and whose conclusions have been uniformly referred to as the 'Jones Report'), there needed to be a clear separation between population policy and immigration policy. Governments should 'understand that establishing a population policy is a *primary* goal and that setting immigration levels is a *secondary* consequence of the population goal'. As the Jones Report put it, 'immigration should not be treated like a tap to be turned on when economic conditions are good and off when they are bad'. This was because 'every increase in population imposes social and environmental costs unless accompanied by the adoption of policies of resource restraint and increased sensitivity about waste disposal, urban structures, and transport modes'.[9] Ideally, population policy should incorporate principles aimed at ensuring that Australia's population was ecologically sustainable and didn't impinge on the nation's quality of life.[10]

Whether such principles have since guided Australian governments is debatable. But the facts can't be disputed: Australia's population has been getting bigger, and it has primarily been driven by increases in immigration. During the past two decades, net overseas migration (the difference between the number who arrive and the number who leave) has been steadily increasing. From a low in the mid-1990s, when the annual figure dipped well below 50 000 as a result of economic recession, net overseas migration has exceeded 100 000 every year in the decade beginning in 2000 and accelerated during the final years of the Howard government. During the Rudd government, net overseas migration peaked at close to 320 000 in the year to March 2009; net overseas migration is estimated to be just over 190 000 for the year to December 2012.[11] Based on the forecasts of the Treasury's Intergenerational Report of 2010, if levels of immigration stabilise, and there is an annual net overseas migration rate of about 180 000, it is likely that Australia's population will reach 26 million by 2020 and 36 million by 2050.[12]

While there isn't the same urgency of 'populate or perish', some consider a larger population still to be a national imperative. The threat that it combats isn't one of military invasion but that of complacency and economic stagnation. As typically presented, the case for a big Australia is based on two arguments, one demographic and one economic. First, it is argued that a larger population would redress the problem of an ageing population. According to Treasury forecasts, there will be only 2.7 people of working age (15–64 years old) to support each Australian aged 65 years and over in 2050, compared to a ratio of 5 to 1 in 2010.[13] Increasing the population would alleviate some of the pressure that a smaller workforce would place on government finances and public services (the fewer people of working age, the fewer there are to pay taxes and, presumably, the harder it will be to meet the cost of providing the standard of public services we enjoy today). Second, proponents of a big Australia suggest that population increases would make it easier for Australia to achieve economic growth. As discussion about 'the Asian Century' reminds us, Australia is well positioned to benefit from the shift of economic power towards Asia. Maintaining a substantial immigration program would, it is argued, strengthen Australia's links with those countries in Asia with which we trade and from which we attract investment.

Offsetting an ageing population and capitalising on an Asian century are weighty reasons for entertaining a bigger Australia. But they seem only to take us so far. It makes no sense to say that more immigrants will keep our population young as any effect that a higher level of immigration makes to the age structure of society will be temporary. Immigrants aren't immune from growing old themselves. In any case, a more measured judgement about an ageing population may be in order. Perhaps we shouldn't assume that a higher proportion of people aged 65 and over means a higher dependency ratio: if people are living longer, and more healthily, it follows that they are also able to work longer. And if an ageing population is indeed a problem, higher immigration isn't the only available response. There is no reason why we shouldn't respond to a shrinking workforce by trying to boost work participation and fertility rates.

The positive economic effects of a larger population are also contested. If Australia has benefited from Asian economic development during the past decade, a big part of it is because we export resources to meet regional demand for coal, iron ore and other minerals. The contribution of a bigger Australia seems to have been marginal: the crucial factor has been demand in Asia. The Sustainable Development Panel, chaired by Bob Carr in 2010 as part of the Commonwealth government's sustainable population strategy, goes much further. There is, in its view, an essentially negligible relationship between population growth and economic growth.[14] Some existing research on the topic indeed suggests that the positive effect of immigration on economic growth is modest at best. One frequently cited study, the Productivity Commission's 2006 report on the economic impacts of migration and population growth, found only a small benefit from higher immigration, measured in terms of gross domestic product per head.[15]

However, such research shouldn't be interpreted as a decisive argument against the economic case for a bigger Australia. The precise economic effects of population growth can be hard to quantify. In the case of the Productivity Commission's findings, the modelling used extended only twenty years out. While that may seem a fair period of time, it mightn't be the most appropriate frame within which to evaluate the economic contribution of immigrants, especially those who arrive in Australia as young workers. Would we, for instance, measure the economic contribution to Australian society of an immigrant such as Frank Lowy, who arrived here in 1952 in his early twenties, only up to the year 1972? Would we value the contributions made by postwar immigrants from Italy and Greece only up until 1980? Where we take a longer view of things, the benefits of population growth are more obvious. Modelling used in the 2010 Intergenerational Report shows that with annual net overseas migration of 180000, the average household in Australia would enjoy a real income of $275000 in today's dollars by 2050 (compared to a mean household income of $86000 in 2007–08). By contrast, a net overseas migration of 70000 would lead to the equivalent of $10000 less in real annual income for every household by 2050.[16]

Nonetheless, any consideration of the economics of immigration needs to go beyond economic modelling.

This is because economic modelling, including that used by the Treasury in the Intergenerational Report, has its limits in capturing the benefits of a larger population. It fails to reflect how some industries would exploit 'economies of scale' in a bigger Australia. The current size of Australia, reinforced by its geographic isolation, means that these are difficult to achieve in many industries. Moreover, it fails to account for how the size of our population affects the quality of competition in the economy. To use economic parlance, a lack of size might reduce competition in the marketplace by acting as a significant 'barrier to entry'. Given a relatively small Australian population, in some industries one or two large firms may be able to meet demand without facing the threat of entry by new competitors. There is a significant concentration of ownership or control in manufacturing, retail, transport, construction, media and banking, to name a few. If we accept that competitive markets usually deliver lower costs, Australia is more likely to suffer from the inefficiencies associated with a small population.[17]

There is also the matter of the 'quest for talent' or the 'battle for brainpower'.[18] Again, this concerns one long-term benefit of immigration that can't be accounted for in even the most sophisticated economic modelling. In a global economy, with mobility of people as well as capital, there is fierce competition between countries (and corporations) to attract highly skilled workers.

Policy-makers understand the benefits of skilled migration. As journalist Philippe Legrain explains, 'talented foreigners may boost innovation, the elixir of long-term economic growth'.[19] In the United States, for example, immigrant scientists and knowledge workers have made a disproportionately high contribution to the information technology boom. Consider the celebrated examples of Taiwanese-born Jerry Yang, the co-founder of Yahoo!, and Russian-born Sergey Brin, the co-founder of Google. It is estimated that the 600 000-odd immigrants admitted into the US between 1992 and 1999 via its H-1B Visa Program (aimed at recruiting workers in specialty occupations) were responsible for the founding of about a quarter of all the companies in Silicon Valley. Similarly, almost a quarter of the founders or chairs of the biotechnology companies that went public in the US during the early 1990s were from abroad. Immigrant knowledge workers have been, in no small measure, responsible for innovations and advances in the US knowledge economy.[20]

So far, Australia has been a keen participant in the contest for global talent. There is a link, though, between brainpower and demography that isn't always well articulated by Australian supporters of higher immigration. Older populations will struggle to be places of economic dynamism – to be the kinds of places that attract international investment. As a result, these populations can struggle to keep their most talented young citizens, who choose to pursue their ambitions elsewhere. Conversely, a society with a growing population, which recruits highly skilled and educated immigrants, can enjoy an economic vigour that draws in further economic activity and people. Capital and global talent tend to cluster. They are pulled towards cities and countries which are energetic and outward-looking. This explains the appeal of global cities like London and New York: globally mobile professionals flock to live in them because they are exciting, diverse and have an international sophistication.

There is a choice, then, that confronts Australia. We could entertain the possibility of Australia remaining more or less static in size. Or we could embrace a larger population, and aspire to make Australia an enticing place for the world's best and brightest. Against the background of an ageing population, potential skills shortages and a competitive quest for global talent, maintaining a relatively high immigration intake would be an important investment in economic prosperity.

What about quality of life?

Not everyone would opt for a bigger Australia. Population stabilisation is the preferred option of environmentalists such as Australian Conservation Foundation president Ian Lowe and activist–businessman Dick Smith. For all its apparent simplicity, what population stabilisation involves in practical terms isn't straightforward. Populations aren't easy to plan, given the variability of factors such as a society's fertility rate. But the case for stabilisation tends to home in on the one thing that governments can plan for: immigration. Assuming that the birthrate remains much the same as the present rate of 1.9 children per adult woman, stabilising Australia's population at its current level of about 23 million would require a reduction of annual net overseas migration to substantially under 70 000 per year.[21] Were net overseas migration to be higher than that, the national population would, in all likelihood, continue to grow. Annual net overseas migration of 70 000, for example, would see the population rise to 25 million by 2020 and to 30 million by 2050.

The case for population stabilisation is well-rehearsed, but has evolved over time. It was once popular to discuss the question of Australia's population 'carrying capacity' – that is, the size of the population that could ecologically be supported. This has much less currency now. 'The search for a magic figure or Rubicon between safety and danger is chimerical', as the Jones Report warned. Quite simply, '[t]here is no numerical population level beyond which the social fabric and environmental quality might be expected to go into precipitate decline'.[22]

The preferred language today is that of sustainable development, which invokes the idea that all Australians can lead a fulfilling life, in a prosperous society, but without degrading the natural environment. In the sustainable development view, progress and well-being should be measured against indicators encompassing the environment (land, water and energy), the health of communities (social services and infrastructure) and the economy (income and wealth). At its heart are two propositions. One is a rejection of the idea that economic growth should be the sole or primary criterion of social progress. Some advocates of sustainable development even suggest that we should try to manage or enjoy prosperity 'without growth', though this is a more radical proposal not endorsed by all opponents of a bigger Australia; many would still accept that rising income and wealth per head of population should remain *one of* the key indicators of progress.[23] The other proposition concerns 'quality of life'. This has become the dominant theme of critiques of population growth and high immigration. According to the Sustainable Development Panel, for example, 'stabilising Australia's population may give Australia the best chance of leaving future Australians a prosperous nation that affords them a high quality of life, living in a healthy and resilient environment'.[24] In similar vein, Lowe argues in favour of 'scaling back immigration [in order] to protect our quality of life'.[25]

What is interesting about these arguments is that the case against population growth is no longer being made in exclusively, or even primarily, ecological terms. Lowe himself acknowledges that 'the limitations on the Australian population this century will be mainly social, rather than the physical constraints of food and water, unless other problems like lack of energy and fertiliser dramatically reduce food production'.[26] Advocates of sustainable development haven't stopped believing that the growth of Australian cities and associated increased consumption will lead to losses in native wildlife and vegetation, to declining availability and quality of water, and indeed to increased greenhouse gas emissions. Yet the emphasis of concern has shifted to the social stresses that population growth during the past two decades has placed on Australian capital cities. Spending on infrastructure, it is argued, hasn't kept pace with population growth. As a result, there is 'a widespread perception that the quality of life in urban areas is deteriorating', especially in outer suburban areas. Such aspects of urban development are tied explicitly to the impact of immigration and also cultural diversity. As Lowe puts it:

> It is ... no coincidence that the recent increase in the level of concern about growth coincides with the shift in the balance between natural increase and migration. The two components of growth had been about equal, on average, for about 40 years. The balance was shifted decisively by the Howard government when it approved a dramatic increase in migration ... There is no doubt that

the size and balance of the migrant intake is
causing social complications. There are benefits
of diversity, but also tensions arising from being
a less homogeneous society. The current rate of
migration from Asia and Africa is causing social
problems in our cities.[27]

Unfortunately, Lowe doesn't elaborate in any length on
the claims that the rate of Asian and African immigration
are causing 'social problems': it is simply assumed that
they exist, and that we know exactly what they are. Such
ambivalence is one troubling feature of environmentalists' arguments against population growth and high
immigration. There are occasions when ecological and
social concerns about population growth seem aligned
with xenophobic populism. Journalist George Megalogenis highlights that 'not all dog whistles are meant
to be heard by the redneck voter in electorates that are
whiter, greyer and poorer than the national average'.
The language of 'sustainable population growth' seems
to resemble a dog whistle aimed at 'the green voter in
electorates that are better educated than the national
average'. According to Megalogenis, the idea is that
while 'the last migrant that came to your street is the
best friend you will ever have [...] the next one is some
filthy-rich son or daughter of Asia's elites who has more
cash than brains, and is bent on sub-dividing the suburb
to build apartment towers'.[28]

The anti-immigrant slant can be more blatant than this, of course. Perhaps the most notable example of extreme 'ecological nationalism' is the now deregistered political party Australians Against Further Immigration, whose members contested seats at state and federal elections on a platform aimed at reducing immigration and preventing an 'Asianisation' of Australia.[29] One of its leaders, Denis McCormack, spoke publicly about the danger of Australia's 'absorption into the teeming masses of Asia' and once brandished the magazine of a machine gun, saying that if immigration wasn't halted, 'it could come to this'.[30]

The sentiments expressed by AAFI are by no means representative of those who oppose a larger Australia on the grounds of sustainability. Yet even moderate, mainstream environmentalist critics of population growth like Lowe can display apparent equivocation about the excesses of eco-nationalism. In reflecting on the 'cultural protectionism' of groups such as AAFI and One Nation, Lowe remarks that suggestions that 'migrants from Asia or Africa are undermining our cultural fabric' constitute 'unexceptionable statements' about immigration's impact on the social fabric. Elsewhere, while rejecting some hardline anti-immigrant sentiment as having little validity in environmental terms, Lowe intimates that the anti-multicultural position of AAFI 'may be a defensible argument in social terms'.[31] It is open to question whether some mainstream articulations of sustainable development may draw upon the cultural elements of an ecological nationalism, if only tacitly.

We shouldn't dismiss environmentally-tinged concerns about the impact of rapid population growth and high immigration on quality of life as a cover for AAFI-style extremism. There is a clearly significant level of discomfort about population growth, which is linked to concerns about maintaining a high quality of life. In their qualitative study of public opinion in 2010, social researchers Rebecca Huntley and Bernard Salt observed that population growth was the issue 'that triggered the most discussion' among their study's participants. The notion of an Australian population approaching 30 million by 2020 'sparked a spectrum of emotions from mild concern to shock and horror'. But as Huntley and Salt reported it, the basic concern was that growth of this kind would overwhelm the infrastructure in cities such as Sydney and Melbourne. As expressed by one participant in their study, 'There's no way we can support any of this growth. If we go to 30 million – no electricity, water, health. Unless they all move out of the cities. It will definitely sink. We'll be in a lot of trouble.'[32]

It is upon quality of life that much of our population debate hinges. The concept has come to resemble something of a trump card. When Gillard sought to assuage public concern about a 'big Australia', she tellingly pledged that she would be 'preserving the quality of life of our Australian sanctuary'.[33] Both supporters of a larger population and sceptics of population growth assume there is an unavoidable trade-off between quality of life and population growth. It seems obvious that a sustained intake of immigrants will have some negative impact on the liveability of our cities: urban density would surely have to increase, and we should all get used to driving on more congested roads and travelling on more crowded trains. That may just be the price we have to pay to enjoy the benefits of a larger population and having genuinely global cities.

It is worth challenging this assumption. After all, much depends on what precisely we mean by quality of life. The term exists as a vehicle for our beliefs about what the good life must involve. The Australian conception of quality of life, at least as it is popularly invoked, is bound up in a cultural way of life befitting the world's 'lifestyle superpower', as BBC correspondent Nick Bryant has memorably described Australia.[34] While, as I argued in Chapter 3, we should take care not to reduce national culture to lifestyle, it remains nonetheless true that part of the national consciousness is tied to the idea of living in a sun-kissed land, with wide open spaces and easy living in the suburbs, in a nation enjoying material and social comfort, insulated from a threatening world. Our intuitive understanding of quality of life reflects a deeply sentimental ideal of 'the Australian dream', of living in houses on quarter-acre blocks with sprawling backyards, where children can play with abandon in sunshine. Not for us those high-rise apartment blocks of dark, polluted metropolises in Asia and elsewhere.

For the most part, the perception of quality of life remains defined by a cultural understanding of what Australia must mean. There's one glaring problem with all of this. An ease of lifestyle isn't the only measure of quality of life. That is one reason why it would make little sense to believe that those who live in the tropical bliss of, say, the Seychelles or the Maldives enjoy the same quality of life as those of us who live in Sydney or Melbourne. Indeed, advocates of a bigger Australia and of population stabilisation alike agree that a good quality of life is composed of a number of things: economic prosperity, access to public services, social cohesion, ecological sustainability. Any assessment of quality of life, in other words, must take into account our welfare or well-being. Understanding quality of life in this way can have profound implications on how we approach questions of population growth and immigration, for it suggests that a basic conflict between population growth and quality of life may not necessarily exist.

Take issues such as urban congestion and density. It is commonly assumed that more crowded cities are a symptom of unsustainable development. This is true, in one sense: where investment in infrastructure doesn't keep up with population growth, there is clearly a problem. Yet this shouldn't be confused to mean that more crowded cities, in and of themselves, mean a diminished quality of life. Higher urban density can be as much a benefit as a cost. It enhances economic dynamism by reducing the costs of production and consumption. It also enriches cultural life by facilitating an easier spread of ideas. It is no accident that the cultural, intellectual and commercial capitals of the world – New York, London, Paris, Shanghai, Mumbai – draw upon a certain scale and concentration of population.[35] Nor is it an accident, perhaps, that of the cities consistently rated the most liveable in the world, just about all have significantly higher population density than Australian capitals. Vienna, rated as the world's most liveable city in Mercer's 2011 annual Quality of Living Survey, has a density that is double that of Sydney (4000 people per square kilometre compared to 2000 people per square kilometre).[36] Vancouver, which over the last decade has been rated consistently by the Economist Intelligence Unit as the world's most liveable city, is almost three times more densely populated than Melbourne (5300 people per square kilometre compared to 1500 people per square kilometre).[37]

Put another way, there can be great diversity in what constitutes a good quality of life. There is no necessary reason to believe that a larger population must mean a reduction in liveability. This isn't to say there are no limits whatsoever to a bigger Australia: an Australia with a population range of 50–100 million people by 2050 would involve very dramatic changes in lifestyle and resource use that would involve an unambiguous decline in quality of life by any definition of the term. But if a 'big Australia' were to mean one with a population of between 30 and 40 million by 2050, that needn't be regarded as the death knell to the Australian way of life – whatever that means. It may come with some costs, but these could be outweighed by the benefits. The key question is whether Australian governments and society can accommodate a larger population while making significant investment in transport infrastructure and housing, and ensuring that it doesn't inflict excessive ecological degradation.

Population policy and multiculturalism

So which population option should Australians choose? And what, if anything, does it have to do with multiculturalism? Let's first be clear about what the population options are, exactly. We can rule out a few possibilities. As noted, no reasonable person – not even those most enthusiastically in favour of a bigger Australia – would seriously suggest that we should aim for a population of say 100 million, or even 50 million, by 2050. Nor would any reasonable person entertain the idea of a reduced Australian population – to turn the clock back two or three decades, or even further, and have a population of substantially lower than 20 million. If we take the projections used in the 2010 Intergenerational Report, the options seem to lie somewhere between population stabilisation (which, based on most reasonable projections, would require annual net overseas migration to be considerably lower than 70 000) and what could be described as the 'extreme big Australia' population option (something like a population of 42 million by 2050, which would involve annual net overseas migration of 300 000). Between these two poles are a moderate-growth option (a population of 30 million by 2050, based on annual net overseas migration of 70 000) and a high-growth option (a population of 36 million, based on annual net overseas migration of 180 000).[38]

Either of the latter two growth options represent the most realistic and appropriate population options for Australia in the long term – preferably the high-growth option. The case for population stabilisation, if it is to be understood in terms of protecting an Australian quality of life, isn't persuasive. There is a strong case for a larger population to address (if only in part) an ageing population and to position Australia for economic prosperity in what is likely to be an Asian century. This shouldn't be understood to mean locking Australia in to a fixed net overseas migration level of 180 000 each year. The level may vary from year to year, depending among other things on economic circumstances. Should there be an economic downturn and a rise in unemployment, for example, it would make sense to accept fewer immigrants until there is a recovery. An explicit population policy isn't a rigid program demanding strict adherence; instead, it outlines a long-term trajectory.

Such a policy geared towards what I've labelled a high-growth option doesn't ignore sustainable development. Any sound argument in favour of population growth needs to account not only for how the natural environment can be adequately looked after, but also for the impact that more people will have on greenhouse gas emissions and climate change.

There is a somewhat counterintuitive possibility in this respect. Planning for a larger population may be an opportunity to introduce significant changes to resource use and lifestyle: a shift towards higher-density cities, with better public transport and less reliance on private cars, and a shift towards more efficient use of energy and resources. In its contemporary form, the suburban 'great Australian dream' lifestyle encourages relatively low residential density and the building of larger homes. The average floor area of the Australian home (which includes houses as well as apartments) is now on average the largest in the world at 214 square metres – more than double the average floor area of homes in Ireland and Sweden, and close to triple the average in the UK.[39] But such residential patterns don't lend themselves to efficiency in the consumption of energy and the use of transportation. Bigger homes, with more rooms, tend to be accompanied by more appliances and be more hungry for power; people in low-density suburbs of detached houses and backyards tend to get around in cars rather than buses, trains or trams. Were population growth and immigration to encourage people to live in homes with average floor sizes of 120 square metres rather 210 square metres, or to live in metropolitan areas that are denser but better serviced by public transport, it may actually contribute to greater sustainability, rather than detract from it. The key to sustainability mightn't be population size as such, but rather how a given population *consumes* resources.

Admittedly, a high-growth option mightn't be politically palatable. The evident discomfort many Australians have with population growth shouldn't be mistaken, however, as committed support for population stabilisation. It is doubtful that Australians would be prepared to accept the full consequences of dramatically reducing immigration levels, once it is appreciated that this would result in a significant drop in economic growth and, potentially, incomes. If Australians should be so thoroughly exercised by modest increases in the cost of living in a period of economic growth they would be unlikely to entertain the consequences of population stabilisation. The economic costs involved aren't trivial. Economists highlight that by 2050 the Australian economy would be 108 per cent larger than in 2009 with annual zero net overseas migration, but it would be 202 per cent larger with annual net overseas migration of 180 000.[40] Amid the ongoing resources boom there remains high demand for labour to construct related infrastructure such as ports, railway lines, pipelines and roads. Beyond this, Australia is embarking on significant investments in infrastructure, such as a national broadband network. Assuming that the resources boom doesn't come to an abrupt halt, cutting back immigration to stabilise our current population would have significant and immediately felt economic consequences.

Moreover, while population growth may well be a 'hot-button' issue, we shouldn't overstate popular hostility towards high immigration and population growth. The Scanlon Foundation surveys, four of which have been conducted since 2007 (with a fifth due to be released later in 2012), consistently indicate that a majority of Australians believe that current levels of immigration are in fact either 'about right' or 'too low'.[41] If there is public concern about population growth, and the contribution that immigration makes to it, it is likely that Australians want to see the rate of population growth slowed down and the level of immigration reduced. This is very different to supporting the stabilisation of Australia's population, and the radical reduction of Australia's immigration program. Such a state of opinion does mean one thing: were a high-growth option to prove too politically difficult for governments to maintain, the alternative isn't to switch to population stabilisation but to adopt policy settings approaching what I've described as a moderate growth option (with annual net overseas migration of 70 000 and a rise in population to 30 million by 2050). Some supporters of population growth might even argue that something closer to a moderate-growth option is desirable, given the likely difficulty of investing suffi-ciently in infrastructure and housing necessary to sup-port a high-growth option. But ideally, such investments would be made — and Australia would be free to ben-efit from the economic and cultural developments that would arise from a population in excess of 30 million in four decades' time.

No explicit population policy should just be about numbers; it should also be attuned to cultural questions. This is where multiculturalism enters the picture. In the most general sense, the challenge of population growth and immigration poses much the same challenge as the idea of a multicultural Australian society once did. It demands that we reflect upon cultural notions of Aus-tralian society, and be prepared to accept that things cannot remain exactly the same forever. The multicul-tural character of Australian society today is something that most of us take for granted or find unexceptionable, but it would have been unthinkable during the 1940s or 50s or 60s. Even in the 1970s, when the idea of mul-ticulturalism was first embraced, its supporters were unlikely to have imagined that Australia would become the society that it is now — one infused with immigrants not only from Europe, but also from Asia and the Pacific, and from Africa and the Americas. Few would have been able to imagine that Australian society would multiply from one with a population of just 7 million in the years immediately after the Second World War to well over

20 million today. Similarly, it may be unthinkable for many Australians today to conceive of an Australia populated by 36 million in forty years' time, with cities such as Sydney and Melbourne being home to 7 or 8 million people. But such changes may just be the next chapter in the story of building the Australian nation.

Population growth would best be achieved if it is accompanied by ongoing support for multiculturalism – as both a social reality and a public policy. Public acceptance of high levels of immigration requires effective policies on the settlement and integration of immigrants. This gets to the heart of one potential source of complacency in the current debate about multiculturalism. It would be foolhardy to believe that the work of any multicultural policy is complete, that immigrant groups have already been successfully incorporated into Australian society and that affirmations of multiculturalism involve unhelpful throwbacks to ethnic identity politics. How, then, are we to settle and integrate new immigrant arrivals? Are we to take for granted that they will follow the same path as previous waves of immigrants in becoming Australians? Can we afford to downplay the importance of negotiating cultural diversity when the majority of immigrants are likely to come from Asia?

The Australian model of multiculturalism has proven, as I've argued, to be highly successful. Any reasonable assessment comparing the Australian experience to those of other liberal democracies would come to this conclusion. As an official policy, multiculturalism outlines a clear path for immigrants to follow in order to become full members of an Australian national community. There is no ambiguity about how Australians should understand immigrants or how immigrants should understand themselves. They're neither guest workers in a host society nor strangers in our midst; they're settlers who in their time shall become fellow citizens, fellow Australians. And in time they will leave their cultural imprint on Australian national identity.

There is one looming challenge to the multicultural citizenship approach to immigrant settlement and integration. During the past decade the numbers of people gaining temporary entry to Australia has increased sharply. There are currently more than a million people living in Australia on a long-term temporary basis, compared to 790 000 in 2004.[42] Of this number, the largest group are current or former international students permitted to remain in Australia for another 18 months (over the past three years to 2010–11, Australia has granted more than 800 000 student visas).[43] The remainder of temporary immigrants consist of working holiday-makers and holders of the '457' skilled worker visas (introduced by the Keating government and formalised by the Howard government to bring in overseas workers to fill in skills gaps in the Australian labour market).

Journalist and writer Peter Mares suggests there has been a 'permanent shift to temporary migrants' which is on a par with other historic developments such as the post–Second World War push for mass immigration from Europe, the abolition of the White Australia policy and the shift towards skilled and business migration since the 1980s. According to Mares, the particular significance lies in the emergence of a new class of labour comprising international students and those on working holidays:

> It may seem odd to include international students and backpackers in a discussion of temporary migrant labour, since, in theory at least, their work in Australia is subsidiary to the primary purpose of studying or holidaying. But, like 457 Visa holders, these temporary workers have come to occupy key sectors in the Australian economy. You need only chat to a Melbourne taxi driver, the person behind the till in a late night convenience [store], the weekend attendant at a petrol station, or the staff stacking supermarket shelves to learn that international students now constitute a significant proportion of the low status, casual workforce in the contemporary service economy. In rural areas, working holidaymakers often provide the key labour force for fruit picking and other seasonal occupations. In tourist areas these travellers often wait in the cafes or hire out the dive equipment.[44]

The rapid growth of temporary migration hasn't been an entirely positive development. There has been justified public concern about the relationship between temporary residence in Australia – particularly in the form of 457 visas and study at universities and other educational institutes – and the granting of permanent residency. In recent years, there has been an implied understanding among many who arrive as temporary immigrants that their initial period in Australia would, as a matter of course, be followed by permanent residency. There were some clearly unsavoury elements involved in how this arrangement played out, as demonstrated by the proliferation of dodgy private providers of further education. Acting on the recommendations of the Knight Review in 2011, the Commonwealth government has since moved to strengthen the integrity of the student visa program.[45] But there remain other questions concerning, for example, the 457 visa program. The Deegan Review into the program in 2008 reported that there were well-founded concerns about the exploitation of temporary immigrant workers, particularly in low-paying jobs.[46] While the government's response to the review included a number of reforms – among other things, a market-based minimum salary for all new and existing 457 visa holders – long-term temporary immigrants arguably remain more vulnerable to exploitation and unfair treatment in the workplace.

We must guard against one potential danger. Australia's immigration program since the Second World War has been unambiguously nation-building in character. The emergence of temporary migration clearly challenges a multicultural approach to settlement and integration, which takes citizenship as its end point for new arrivals. Where immigrants are understood as temporary visitors rather than permanent settlers, the risk is that it becomes easier to regard them as, well, guest workers. Granted, temporary migration will exist into the future, to some degree – and that is a good thing. We should welcome the arrival of international students to Australian universities, particularly as it helps to strengthen our relations with neighbouring countries in Asia. But temporary migration of the sort allowed under the 457 visa should exist only to the extent that it is necessary to respond to short-term labour shortages. It shouldn't be used to allow Australian employers to exploit vulnerable international workers, with the effect of undercutting Australian working conditions. It shouldn't create a caste of 'permanently temporary' workers who live here for long periods of time, contribute to our economy and society, but are unable to settle here permanently.

What must be rejected are proposals such as the one made by billionaire mining magnate Gina Rinehart for the creation of special, low-tax economic zones that would be powered by a labour force of foreign guest workers. Rinehart, who in February 2012 put her thoughts into a poem titled 'Our Future', argues that we should 'Develop North Australia, embrace multiculturalism and welcome short term foreign workers to our shores/To benefit from the export of our minerals and ores'.[47]

Of course, Rinehart's wish has since been partially granted. In May 2012, the Gillard government announced it had reached an 'enterprise migration agreement' with Rinehart's Hancock Prospecting company to construct the Roy Hill iron ore mine in the Pilbara. Under the agreement, some 1700 temporary foreign workers would be allowed to work on the $9.5 billion project, as part of a workforce projected to be as large as 8400. As this book went to press, there remain many details about the Roy Hill agreement that aren't known: EMAs are confidential 'deeds of agreement', the full contents of which won't be publicly disclosed. But there is enough for some to be concerned that they may amount to a way for mining companies to introduce 'cheap foreign labour' at the expense of Australian jobs and workers' rights. There was much heated rhetoric, involving a healthy dose of protectionism if not also thinly veiled racism, in response to the Roy Hill announcement. Labor senator Doug Cameron warned of 'marching Chinese workers' on to the Pilbara; his federal parliamentary colleague Kelvin Thomson fulminated that EMAs 'will see foreign companies using foreign workforces to send irreplaceable, once only resources, in foreign ships, to foreign countries, for the use and enjoyment of foreign consumers'.[48]

The potential problem with EMAs, at least in the

current economic environment, doesn't concern foreign workers taking Australian jobs as such. Unemployment remains low – remarkably so when compared to other OECD countries. There are very real skills shortages in the mining sector. Ostensibly, there aren't as many workers in the eastern states who are prepared to move their families to take on mining jobs, especially in remote parts of Western Australia, as we might assume. But if there are structural labour shortages, why aren't these being filled with permanent skilled immigrants rather than temporary ones? Shouldn't we think twice before conducting an immigration policy with attention only to short-term economic needs?

We should avoid at all costs a program of immigration that devalues political membership. American political philosopher Michael Walzer puts it like this: where a country lets in an immigrant, they must be open to ensuring they are free to settle permanently and become citizens, with all the rights that come with full membership. 'Democratic citizens', as he argues, 'have a choice: if they want to bring in new workers, they must be prepared to enlarge their own membership; if they are unwilling to accept new members, they must find ways within the limits of the domestic labour market to get socially necessary work done. And those are their only choices.'[49] Increasingly, however, we seem to be choosing a third way: a citizenship model in name that is growing dependent upon temporary immigrants. If we have learned anything from the experience of guest workers in democracies such as Germany, that is one addiction Australia would be better off without.

5

The sovereignty of fear

In his fiction anthology *The Boat*, expatriate Australian writer Nam Le concludes with a poignant story about Vietnamese refugees, crammed on to a boat, journeying through rough seas. After twelve days, seemingly adrift, they finally sighted land. A 'swell of excitement' ran through the boat. 'We made it,' one of the boat people announces. 'We're safe now.' Yet the elation is momentary. It soon emerges that another of their number – a small boy, Truong – has perished in the hold below the deck. With a blurry peninsula in sight, those on the boat give Truong his burial at sea, standing together in silence at the prow.[1]

Thirty-five years ago, Hieu Van Le made a similar boat trip from the southern tip of Timor to Australia, aboard what he describes as 'a small, flimsy fishing boat'. He had been on the seas for nearly a month since fleeing Vietnam; this would be the last leg of his fateful journey. On the third day crossing the Timor Sea, there was some excitement on deck – someone had spotted seagulls, a sure sign that they were close to land. As Le recalls, the boat shortly after sailed into Darwin harbour. With nervous apprehension, he and his 39 fellow refugees watched as the buzz of an outboard motor approached the boat:

> Gradually, emerging out of the morning mist, we saw a 'tinnie', with two blokes with shorts and singlets in it, sun hats on, white zinc cream on their noses, fishing rods primed and sticking up in the air and the first beers of the day were in their hands …They waved at us and steered their boat very close to ours, and one of them raised his stubby as if proposing a toast. 'G'day, mate,' he shouted. 'Welcome to Australia!' Then he revved up the motor and sped off to get on with the fishing trip they set out to do. We have never seen them again.[2]

It was obviously a much happier ending than that experienced by the characters of Nam Le's *The Boat*. Hieu Van Le today is Lieutenant Governor of South Australia and Chairman of the South Australian Multicultural and Ethnic Affairs Commission. Reflecting upon his introduction to Australia, he remains amazed at the 'warmth and good nature of this laconic welcome'. What greeted him was 'a remarkable generosity of spirit'.

Of course, the reception hasn't been universally pleasant for refugees. Many would say there is fear and loathing of those who arrive in Australia by boat.

Vietnamese and other Indochinese refugees weren't by any means immune to this, but whereas they had the relative comfort of migrant hostels, more recent boat arrivals have had to contend with harsher conditions. Following the introduction of mandatory detention in the early 1990s, asylum seekers who arrived in Australia by boat were sent to compounds in remote locations such as Port Hedland, Curtin, Baxter and Woomera. Men, women and children often spent years living behind steel fences and razor wire before learning the result of their asylum claims. The despair of living in such conditions, with fates unknown, sent many into hunger strikes and riots.[3] While periodic unrest within outback detention centres convinced many Australians of the inhumane nature of mandatory detention, it convinced others of the threatening character of asylum seekers.

It wasn't until the events of 2001 that Australian public hostility towards asylum seekers entered a new phase. The *Tampa* incident and the so-called 'children overboard' incident led to a dramatic hardening of sentiment against asylum seekers. The two incidents are, by now, infamous. At the end of August, the Norwegian freighter MV *Tampa* rescued at Australia's request some 400-odd Afghan asylum seekers from a stricken boat in the Indian Ocean, with instructions to take them back to Indonesia. When the asylum seekers insisted that *Tampa* continue on to Australia, Special Air Service troops were dispatched to ensure that it wouldn't. Following

Tampa, all asylum seekers travelling to Australia by boat were intercepted and had their claims for asylum processed offshore in Christmas Island, Nauru and Manus Island in Papua New Guinea – the so-called Pacific solution. Not long after the *Tampa* episode, in October 2001, the 'children overboard' incident took place. The Howard government alleged that asylum seekers aboard a wooden-hulled boat ('SIEV 4'), which sank north of Christmas Island, had thrown their children overboard in order to entice Australian authorities to tow them to land (a 2002 Senate inquiry into the affair found that no children had been at risk of being thrown overboard).

Through *Tampa* and 'children overboard', the Howard government ensured two things: that boat arrivals would be dramatically politicised as an issue of border protection, and that asylum seekers would be demonised as desperate, immoral opportunists willing to do anything to make it to Australia, even willing to risk the welfare of their young. In case the message was lost on the electorate, Howard campaigned for office using the slogan 'We will decide who comes to this country and the circumstances in which they come'. In 2001, Howard set the tone, and the electorate followed him.[4]

More than ten years on, and fuelled by promises on both sides of politics to 'stop the boats' and 'break the business model of people-smuggling', it is easy to detect continued widespread hostility towards boat people. But it is the manner in which boat arrivals are routinely used to whip up public frenzy that is most disconcerting. Politicising the issue of asylum may have dangerous consequences for social cohesion and trust in a multicultural society. Where politicians appeal to notions of national sovereignty to fuel their populism, the result can be a form of national identity not inclusive of cultural diversity. Whether we can conduct a more sober public conversation about asylum seekers and boat arrivals will be an important test of Australia's multicultural maturity.

The politics of asylum and boat people

An outsider to this country could be forgiven for finding it odd that so much public debate is generated by the arrival of asylum seekers, particularly those who reach our shores by boat. The outsider would be struck, first of all, by the disproportionate concern about asylum seekers as a matter of border security. As a geographically isolated island-continent, Australia has an imposing natural barrier to any foreign arrivals by sea. This isn't the impression one gets from our public discourse. The seas and oceans are but puddles over which determined 'illegal immigrants' jump to reach Australia. News reports and opinion columns in Sydney's *Daily Telegraph* and Melbourne's *Herald Sun*, for example, are regularly splashed with headlines forecasting that the 'floodgates' will open to a 'deluge' of boat people, or observing that

Australians are 'powerless to stop an invasion of boat people'.[5] This kind of language isn't limited to the tabloid press but is also common used by politicians. Not long after becoming federal opposition leader in 2009, Tony Abbott publicly argued that harsh policies such as mandatory detention and the turning around of boats 'might be necessary to prevent a form of peaceful invasion'.[6] He has only grown more forceful in his determination to 'stop the boats'.

Parochialism can lead some of us to forget that Australia isn't the only country in the world that has to deal with the irregular arrival of immigrants. Some 500 000 unauthorised immigrants are estimated to slip through American borders each year, mainly through its southern frontier with Mexico, with 800 000 thought to make it into Europe annually.[7] When considered alongside such figures, the number of asylum seekers who arrive in Australia by boat hardly warrants comparison. But many believe that a large proportion of Australia's overall migration program is composed of asylum seekers granted refugee protection. For example, the Scanlon Foundation's survey of attitudes in 2011 found that only 23 per cent of respondents correctly estimated the proportion of permanent immigrant arrivals who arrived by boat as asylum seekers. It would come as a surprise to most Australians that in 2010–11 the Commonwealth government had planned for an intake of 13 750 people under its humanitarian program, as part of a net overseas migration estimated to be 170 300 people, and that only approximately 2700 of the humanitarian intake were 'irregular maritime arrivals'.[8] Barrister Julian Burnside, writing in 2011, highlights that at the current rate at which unauthorised boats are arriving in Australia, it would still take 20 years to fill the Melbourne Cricket Ground with asylum seekers.[9]

There is another reason why our outsider might be baffled by the national preoccupation with boat arrivals and a supposed peaceful invasion by asylum seekers. Isn't this, after all, the country that in the late 1970s took in tens of thousands of refugees fleeing the turmoil in Indochina? And wasn't it this development that gave 'substance' to the transition from a white Australia to a multicultural one, as Malcolm Fraser put it? In retrospect, given the relatively successful integration of the Indochinese refugees and their families into society, it is hard to believe that the Fraser government was warned by the Department of Immigration at the time that the situation 'has all the ingredients for one of the most controversial and divisive issues in Australia's history'.[10] But, at the time, it was far from certain that an intake of Indochinese refugees could be managed without major social disruption. That things did turn out this way was a product of a number of factors. Given that Australians had fought alongside the forces of South Vietnam, there was a direct moral obligation to take in refugees who were displaced by the war – a point that seemed to have been appreciated by the Australian public. Any public concern about accepting Vietnamese refugees might also have been allayed by the fact that the Fraser government embarked on an offshore program of resettlement. Of those who were resettled in Australia, about 56 000 refugees came via processing conducted in camps across southeast Asia (combined with subsequent family reunion arrivals, the total becomes 190 000).[11] 'The key to this Australian triumph,' Paul Kelly writes, 'was converting the intake from onshore to offshore'.[12]

Without denying this point, there was one other reason why Indochinese refugees were resettled without much rancour, which also explains much of the success of Australia's multicultural reality over the past three or so decades: both major political parties agreed not to play politics with race. From the time a planned migration program was introduced in Australia during the post–Second World War period, bipartisanship of a certain kind could be taken for granted. Neither side of politics would seek to make political mileage from immigration issues. The stakes were regarded as too high. This bipartisan consensus broke down in the 1990s. Many would say that this coincided with the impact of Pauline Hanson's One Nation, though scholars such as Chandran Kukathas and William Maley astutely highlight that a 'soft Hansonism' was already common in the positions of both Labor and Coalition parties even before Hanson's emergence.

With respect to asylum, a 'persistently negative attitude' towards asylum seekers was given expression through the introduction of mandatory detention in 1992 as a deterrent to boat arrivals.[13] For example, Labor Senator Jim McKiernan, who served as chair of the Joint Standing Committee on Migration, went so far as to claim that if 'the refugee assessment procedure was changed, Australia would be inundated, and boats filled with people, who can afford the fare and the bribes that go with it, will land on our shores by the score'.[14] But it can't be denied that 'hard Hansonism' had a palpable effect on public attitudes. Hanson herself proposed that those proven to be refugees should only be afforded temporary sanctuary from persecution in their homelands – a proposal that would be given effect in the Howard government's adoption of temporary protection visas. Those in favour of a more sympathetic approach to asylum seekers found themselves increasingly denigrated for being complicit in a 'multicultural industry'. Hansonism, and its subsequent appropriation by Howard's aspirational nationalism, made it acceptable to politicise asylum seekers as part of a broader debate about multiculturalism, political correctness and national identity.

Indeed, since the *Tampa* incident we have seen a more nakedly brutal political contest over asylum seeker policy. Much like the issue of 'law and order', political parties seek to outbid each other on how strong they are on maritime national security and how ruthless they are towards people smugglers. Even a Prime Minister like Kevin Rudd, someone who had campaigned for an end to the Pacific solution and for a more compassionate approach to asylum seekers, sought to emphasise a 'tough but humane' stance on the issue while infamously calling people smugglers 'scum of the earth who can rot in hell'.[15] Politicians from both major parties feel that any retreat from a hardline stance on unauthorised boat arrivals will result in savage electoral punishment. They are mindful of the apparent fear that voters have about asylum-seeking boat people. A Lowy Institute poll in 2011, for instance, found that 86 per cent of respondents believed that boat people 'pose a potential security threat to Australia'.[16]

The source of negative concern about asylum seekers is fiercely debated. Many would say it is simply racism. According to Perera, fear of boat people exists because 'secreted in the crevices and dark, invisible spaces of these illegalised bodies and intruding small craft lurk the invading germs and threatening microorganisms of the tropics – that dangerous geography that the very construct of insular Australia strives to hold at bay'.[17] Political historian Robert Manne puts it in more concrete terms: were the majority of asylum seekers white Zimbabwean farmers and their families fleeing from the regime of Robert Mugabe, rather than Afghan Hazaras or Iraqis, it would be 'improbable, or so it seems to me, that public opinion would have tolerated their detention behind razor wire or their transportation to the hellhole in Nauru'.[18]

But not everyone who supports a hardline approach to boat arrivals is motivated by a xenophobic fear of Third-World-looking people. For many, even the harshest or most draconian means of 'stopping the boats' is justified by the risk of death or injury that boat-borne asylum seekers face. Asylum seekers are, on this view, the victims of exploitation by criminal people smugglers and we should do whatever we can to stop the trade. Some Australians believe that a softer stance towards boat arrivals offends the idea of a 'fair go', by having the possible effect of disadvantaging refugees already awaiting resettlement in camps overseas. Boat arrivals also appear to be a proxy for anxieties about population growth and quality of life, as noted in Chapter 4. Clearly, race hasn't been the only factor.

Whatever the reason behind people's anxiety, the politics around border security since *Tampa* has had one unfortunate and troubling effect: it has thoroughly dehumanised asylum seekers. It has become acceptable now, particularly for those favouring a policy of turning boats back, to withdraw empathy from those arriving on boats seeking sanctuary. This involves nothing less than a profound ethical failure.

Here, I should declare my own partiality. It is only natural that my view is shaped by my own parents' experience as refugees. My parents were one of the hundreds of thousands who fled Laos following the communist Pathet Lao's seizure of power in 1975. It is estimated that more than 10 per cent of Laos's population of 3 million left as refugees in the decade after the communist revolution. My mother had the misfortune of being related to a number of army generals aligned with the old royalist regime. She and my father made their way into a crowded refugee camp in north-east Thailand. My mother engaged a people smuggler to transport her across the Mekong River; my father ended up swimming across to Thailand after a dinghy he was aboard was fired upon by Lao border guards along the river bank. Once in Thailand, they lived with more than a dozen others in a small, one-room bamboo hut for several months, in a makeshift village of several thousand refugees. With characteristic understatement, they describe the period as uncertain and difficult. They were lucky to be resettled in France (where I was born), before eventually moving to Australia as immigrants under the family reunion scheme.

In thinking through the ethics of how we should treat asylum seekers, I have often imagined what it would have been like in the position of my parents; how it would have felt to have experienced persecution, and to seek protection from foreign powers in the knowledge that being returned to their homeland would result in a grave fate. My parents had friends who, upon being caught trying to flee Laos, were sent to re-education compounds in the Lao countryside, euphemistically labelled 'seminar' camps. Some would eventually re-emerge after a decade; others who tried to leave the 'seminar' didn't escape with their lives.

But you don't need to be the child of refugees to step into the shoes of an asylum seeker. After all, empathy is a central component of moral reasoning. The modern idea of empathy – the notion of relating to the experience of another person by mirroring it in one's mind – has its roots in the older notion of sympathy. Thus for Scottish philosopher David Hume, sympathy was ultimately 'the foundation of morals'.[19] His contemporary Adam Smith, another elder of the Scottish Enlightenment, similarly placed moral importance on sympathy: an individual should adopt the perspective of the 'impartial spectator', one who can project themselves into another's world so as to conceive what they would feel in a like situation. Only then, Smith argued, could an individual be in a position to make a sound moral judgement.[20] Contemporary Australia seems a rather long way from the Scottish Enlightenment. With the escalating politicisation of asylum, there has emerged the view that any empathy towards boat people may in fact corrupt our moral judgement.

Consider some of the sentiments expressed in the SBS program *Go Back To Where You Came From*. In the program's first season in 2011, six Australians were taken on a journey to recreate the experiences of refugees who have come to Australia (the program's second season hadn't yet screened as this book went to press). Participants lived with refugees who had been resettled here, and then with asylum seekers overseas waiting for their claims to be processed. They saw refugee camps up close. They observed a government raid on asylum seekers in Malaysia. They briefly experienced life on a leaky boat at sea. But, at one point, not long after the program's participants had been rescued from an apparently sinking fishing boat, one of them protested. It was Darren Hassan, a 42-year-old former soldier and aspiring Liberal Party politician. Hassan, visibly upset, challenged the program's producers: the exercise, he said, was eliciting his empathy without consent. It was a revealing moment, which seemed to illustrate that a sangfroid position on boat arrivals could be maintained only as long as one wasn't confronted with the possibility that asylum seekers were real people genuinely fleeing from human suffering.

As if to underscore the point, Hassan's confrontation with producers spurred some hardliners on asylum seekers into taking an even harder line. Conservative commentator Paul Sheehan wrote that *Go Back To Where You Came From* involved 'an empathy forced march'. According to Sheehan, any insertion of empathy into the ethical equation leads to a distortion of the boat people issue:

The empathy argument is easily turned on its head, something the producers [of *Go Back To Where*

You Came From] carefully avoid doing. Far from lacking empathy, the decision to send a punitive signal to the people smugglers and their clients has been proven to stop the people-smuggling trade. Detention centres, instead of being opened all over the country, would empty out. Lives would not be lost at sea. Hundreds of millions of dollars would be spent on people instead of policing. More refugees could come to Australia under less stress and for less cost ... Because this debate is not about empathy. It is not about numbers. It is not about race. It is about principle: control the borders. The biggest beneficiaries of strict border control would be legitimate asylum seekers.[21]

From a multicultural perspective, removing empathy from the equation has two effects. First, recall that multiculturalism demands of us an ethos of public dialogue: we must be prepared to be open to the perspectives of others. Wouldn't a withdrawal of empathy from asylum seekers make such an ethos harder to realise? If we aren't willing even to consider how things might look like from the position of those who are in most cases genuinely vulnerable, it is difficult to see how we would be capable of negotiating cultural diversity in the way I've outlined in previous chapters. Second, and more fundamentally, we can end up being indifferent to human suffering — among the gravest offences possible in a civilised liberal society. Where empathy is no longer a consideration, the discussion of boat people becomes framed as simply a matter of national sovereignty and self-determination.

The corollary is that boat people can be regarded as merely 'illegal immigrants', determined to flout a nation-state's established procedures for determining who is to be admitted into its territory.[22] This has been the ultimate result of the politicisation of asylum seekers. The question of boat arrivals has been turned into a political problem to be solved, it seems, without any consideration for the humanity of the situation. There has been little generosity of spirit. After all, as Sheehan and others would insist, there are principles at stake.

Human rights and membership

But what about a moral principle that we should provide sanctuary to those fleeing persecution? Shouldn't human rights count for something?

The legal obligations that Australia owes to asylum seekers are clear. We are, as a country, one of the signatories to the 1951 Refugee Convention, which enshrines certain rights to those with 'a well-founded fear of being persecuted for reasons of race, religion, nationality, membership of a particular social group or political opinion'. The Convention binds its signatories not to impose penalties on those seeking asylum on account of their mode of entry or lack of authorisation. Article 33 of the

Convention imposes a duty of 'non-refoulement', which states that a refugee shall not be repatriated to their homeland if their lives or freedoms are threatened. In practice, though, the manner in which signatory nations give effect to such duty varies. Many have adopted what refugee scholar Matthew Gibney has called a form of 'organised hypocrisy'. That is, 'liberal democratic states publicly avow the principle of asylum but use fair means and foul to prevent as many asylum seekers as possible from arriving on their territory where they could claim its protections'.[23]

One reason is that the machinery supporting the international protection for refugees was the product of a very different world. It was devised in the years immediately following the Second World War, with the horrors of the Holocaust still fresh. The drafters of the Convention wouldn't have anticipated the scale of the global refugee population that exists today: the UN High Commissioner for Refugees estimated in 2010 that there were some 43 million people who could be considered refugees (a figure that includes people displaced within their own country).[24] Nor would they have anticipated the 'globalisation of asylum', the fact that the spread of air travel has made it easy for people fleeing strife and persecution in places like Sri Lanka, Iraq, Afghanistan and Somalia to reach liberal democracies in the West.[25]

The case of Germany offers an especially powerful illustration of the practical difficulties involved in protecting the rights of asylum seekers. Following the Second World War, West Germany adopted as its constitution 'the Basic Law', which enshrined the principle that 'Persons persecuted on political grounds shall enjoy the right to asylum'. It was a deliberately wide interpretation of a right to asylum, reflecting West Germany's founders' conviction that there would never again be mistreatment of refugees on German soil. During the 1950s and 60s the number of people seeking to exercise a right to asylum on German territory was small, averaging about 5000 a year. This quickly changed in 1980, as a result of civil wars in Turkey, Sri Lanka, Lebanon and elsewhere. The fall of the Berlin Wall in 1989, along with the crisis in Yugoslavia, would see further influxes of asylum seekers. Increasingly, the asylum clause in Germany's constitution served to attract arrivals by supposed refugees with obviously weak claims for asylum, but who nonetheless had every reason to make an application to start a new life in the West. By 1992, the number of annual applications for asylum had risen to 438 000. As philosopher Andy Lamey concludes in his recent book on the global refugee crisis, eventually the Basic Law's asylum clause's 'most powerful effect proved to be negative, when it created an incentive for economic migrants to file unfounded asylum claims'. The experiment of enshrining a constitutional right to asylum 'must be judged a failure'.[26] In 1993, the German Parliament, after a 13-hour debate, voted to radically reform Germany's asylum law: its generous, legal protection of asylum seekers was consigned to history.

If there is a duty owed by political states to protect refugees, it clearly can't be an unqualified one. This seems to be the lesson of the German experience and the experiences of other European countries, such as France and Italy, which introduced an asylum clause in their post–Second World War constitutions. For all of the universalism that attaches itself to the language of human rights, any protection afforded to asylum seekers remains shaped by political realities. What is a universal right in theory may be a somewhat limited one in practice.

This asymmetry reflects a philosophical and political tension between human rights and national sovereignty. In a globalising world, communities are confronted with a choice between a universalism that makes no distinction between members and strangers, and a particularism that takes national self-determination seriously. For cosmopolitan universalists, we are simply citizens of the world. Our citizenship shouldn't be defined by our membership of national communities.[27] Whether Afghan or Australian, Sri Lankan or Swedish, we are all entitled to equal, non-negotiable rights of liberty and security; these should trump any right that nations have to territorial integrity. Applied to asylum seekers, the cosmopolitan case places a presumptive burden on developed nations to relax their claims to territorial rights and accept more refugees. Anything less would involve a moral crime. Thus, border controls in the US, Europe and Australia effectively involve waging a war on migrants whose only crime is to aspire to a Western way of life.[28] In the Australian context, the cosmopolitan human rights argument is often merged with anti-racism. One constant refrain, as we know, is that any robust stance on border security involves a dog-whistling throwback to a paranoid White Australia or Fortress Australia mentality.

As applied to asylum seekers and refugees, it is unclear how such universalism can pass the test of practical feasibility. A cosmopolitan argument which emphasises the fundamental moral equality of human beings struggles to account for the significance of membership in a particular state or community.[29] Yet national membership still matters for the vast majority of people. Any discussion of distributive justice, encompassing decisions on how to allocate resources or share social goods, presupposes a notion of membership. What we do with membership – whom we decide to admit, and how – shapes all our other distributive choices.[30] A democratic value of political self-determination means that a community should have the right to exercise sovereignty over its borders. Any right of protection that refugees are entitled to enjoy requires co-operating nation-states to give it effect. The only scenario in which this wouldn't be the case would be a world in which nationality has no ethical and political significance; a world in which there are open borders, with the free movement of peoples.

We shouldn't make the mistake of thinking that being sympathetic to cultural diversity or to refugees means that we should support the radical idea of open borders. A multicultural approach exists firmly within a framework of national self-determination. It presumes a contract between citizens and their government – one in which an immigration program accords with a community's national aspirations. In historical terms, Australian public acceptance of mass immigration has been contingent on nation-building ambition. For example, during the past decade Australia has sustained high numbers of immigrants in part because there has been a points-based system of admission geared towards meeting the needs of our growing economy. During the Howard years, some even argued that a strong border protection regime was a prerequisite of a strong overall migration intake. But as debates about population growth reveal, even a period of strong public acceptance of high immigration and cultural diversity can conceal some social strains. Imagine, then, the result if Australia were to adopt an extreme cosmopolitan approach or to go the path of open borders. There are good reasons to limit the assistance a state must provide to refugees. There may be a certain point beyond which the admission of refugees would undermine the trust and solidarity necessary for a functioning polity – not least a multicultural one where trust and solidarity are at a premium.

The matter isn't as simple as affirming the primacy of human rights. This is because rights are the property of citizens. It is citizenship that confers the right to have rights, as philosopher Hannah Arendt wrote. There is a clear and consequential distinction between citizens and foreigners. Citizens enjoy certain rights and protections that foreigners do not. What makes a refugee vulnerable is precisely that they, for whatever reason, can no longer count on their government defending such rights as they possess. The most powerful claim they make is that of humanity, what Arendt called 'the abstract nakedness of being human'.[31] Whatever the moral resonance of such an appeal, it will always be difficult to enforce the rights of asylum seekers and refugees against communities that are resolved to exclude them.

Where does this leave us? Many assume, mistakenly, that a particularistic approach to questions of immigration leaves no room for considerations of justice for outsiders. But self-determination isn't code for 'rule of the mob'. To endorse it isn't to endorse the idea that a political community should merely follow the lead of public opinion on questions of whom to admit within its borders. It is only to say that we recognise the value that people in a community place on having a model of membership that they regard as legitimate. At the very minimum, a liberal nation-state has a general responsibility to uphold basic human rights – it must be willing to accept refugees whose basic rights have been violated or are at risk of being so.[32] One helpful guide is the 'humanitarian principle', which holds that states have an obligation to assist refugees when the cost of doing so is low. States should accept 'as many refugees as they can without undermining the provision of collective or public goods amongst their members'.[33] For Australia, the notion of national sovereignty can't justly be invoked to close off certain obligations which we have willingly entered into as a country. By willingly choosing to sign the Refugee Convention, 'Australia proudly said yes to refugees and yes to asylum seekers fleeing persecution'.[34] In any case, if a debate about asylum seekers is to be guided in part by notions of popular national sovereignty, and by implication notions of national values, an Australian community must take seriously an ethos of fairness or a 'fair go'. Such an ethos would mean little if we are incapable of extending it to those most vulnerable.

Public debate and policy

It is frequently the case that the tone of public debate on an issue will tend to be reflected in public policy, and vice versa. The debate about asylum seekers, being preoccupied with boat arrivals, is often conducted without any sense of proportion: a dubious panic surrounds the relentless talk about stopping the boats and getting tough on people smugglers. With the introduction of mandatory detention and offshore processing, public policy has become increasingly punitive towards asylum seekers. On both counts, what we see is deeply unedifying, and we shouldn't underestimate the effect they have on Australian society. Few would dispute that the policy of mandatory detention for boat arrivals has a harmful impact on the prospects of refugees integrating into Australian society. Whether it has long-term effects on social cohesion and trust in a multicultural society remains to be seen, but you might suspect that the impact of a polarised public debate on asylum seekers isn't positive. Where politicians and citizens don't hesitate to score political points off boat people, it is only too easy to entertain scoring points off immigrants, or anyone else who appears different from the mainstream.

The progressive case for a more humane approach to debate and policy has often faltered because it fails to accept that the world can't be ruled by 'ideal theory'. Sometimes advocating ideas from the vantage point of a perfect ideal – universal human rights – can end up deflecting attention from what may actually be feasible here and now in the real world. In the case of Australia's treatment of asylum seekers, it mightn't be enough to argue that we should simply abandon mandatory detention and offshore processing policies because they are immoral. Since there is no longer a bipartisan readiness to abstain from politicking over questions of immigration, any political party that takes the moral high ground risks being punished electorally for doing so. It would certainly be courageous for either of the major political parties to challenge the Australian public's concern about the spontaneous arrival of asylum seekers on boats. Any move to put a more morally sound policy into practice carries an additional risk: it could have the effect of hardening public hostility towards asylum seekers and encouraging an escalation of populist hysteria.[35]

But accepting the need for realism needn't mean an abandonment of moral principles. It is possible to have a realistic yet morally sound asylum seeker policy which is guided by two principles: empathy and national self-determination.

The possible role of empathy should be obvious. In particular, it is difficult to find a morally persuasive argument in favour of prolonged mandatory detention. While it may be justified as a measure aimed at deterring boat arrivals, the evidence suggests that it doesn't have any such effect.[36] The one possible counterargument – that mandatory detention is necessary for public safety – doesn't appear to hold up. Other countries, including many which receive a far higher number of asylum seeker arrivals, adopt alternatives to mandatory detention; Australia is the only country in the world to pursue a policy of mandatory detention for all asylum seekers who arrive by boat.

Consider also the raw human cost of detention as it is currently practised, which can involve being held in a detention centre without trial, and without any clearly defined time limit. Stories of hunger strikes, self-harm and rioting in detention centres, some of which are located in remote desert areas of Australia, reflect the sense of desperation incarceration can breed. Public health experts have described mandatory detention as a recipe for mental illness, especially among child detainees.[37] If we were, in a philosophical sense, to adopt the perspective of Smith's 'impartial observer', and seek to conceive what we ourselves should feel in that situation before coming to a moral judgement, we would in all likelihood conclude that mandatory detention can't be morally justified.

A transition to a more humane detention policy would be a welcome change. This needn't mean that all forms of detention must be abolished: there are good commonsense reasons to use it in order to conduct health, identity, character and safety assessments of all asylum seekers. But, as recommended by the a parliamentary Joint Select Committee on Australia's Immigration Detention Network, any detention of asylum seekers should be for a defined period, limited to 90 days. Where asylum seekers do pass those basic tests, they should be granted a bridging visa or moved to community detention.[38] Some recent developments indicate that the Gillard government has been making further efforts to ensure a more humane regime. For example, in May 2012 the Gillard government announced that Australian families who opted to participate in a home-stay scheme for asylum seekers on bridging visas could receive up to $300 a week in government support (the Coalition's Immigration Shadow Minister Scott Morrison condemned the move as reckless and potentially dangerous).[39]

As for a principle of national self-determination, its application raises two sets of questions concerning the processing of asylum claims: one about numbers and one about method. On numbers, the national ethos of a 'fair go' surely demands that Australia admit far more refugees in its migration program than is presently the case. As noted earlier, Australia's annual humanitarian program within its migration program stands at about 13 750. While Australia currently takes in more refugees per head of population among the 23 countries that resettle refugees in coordination with UNHCR, there remains considerable scope for a more generous humanitarian program. The Nordic countries of Denmark, Sweden, Norway, Finland and Iceland, for example, whose combined population of 25 million isn't much larger than Australia's 23 million, process about 50 000 asylum claims annually.[40]

The more contentious issue is the method by which asylum claims by those who arrive in Australian territory by boat are processed. The question here is whether this should be done 'onshore' (on the Australian mainland) or 'offshore' (if not on Australian territories such as Christmas Island, then in another country such as Papua

New Guinea or Nauru, which agrees to accept asylum seekers). The most ideal response to the arrival of boat people would be to process their asylum claims 'onshore'. Australia is a signatory to the Refugee Convention and should allow people to have their claims for protection processed on the Australian mainland. But moving to an onshore regime would be best achieved with bipartisan political support. If such a policy shift were to occur, it would be likely to lead to an increase in the number of boat people seeking to make it to Australian territory. In such a scenario, political leaders must be prepared to avoid politicising boat arrivals in a way that inflames public opinion. Where resolve of this kind is missing, a shift to onshore processing may carry the risk of undermining public acceptance of a substantial, non-racially-discriminatory immigration program, and indeed of a multicultural Australian society.

Given the current shape of Australian domestic politics, it is exceedingly unlikely that we will see genuine bipartisanship of this sort emerge any time soon. Yet, short of resolute bipartisanship, a shift to onshore processing is politically unfeasible – as noted, it would likely result in an electoral backlash against any sponsoring major political party. We may rightly lament this, but then we shouldn't forget that politics remains the art of the possible. A realistic assessment would concede that, at least for some time to come, offshore processing of refugee claims will have to play some role in the mix of policies towards asylum seekers. The Australian population appears to prefer the claims of asylum seekers to be processed offshore rather than onshore.

Many friends of asylum seekers don't like offshore processing for an obvious reason: it may be a way for liberal democratic states to avoid their humanitarian obligations. This needn't be the case. There's another way of understanding how offshore processing might fit into the bigger picture of refugee protection. Lamey, for example, proposes what he terms a 'portable-procedural' model of rights for asylum seekers. Under this model, asylum seekers are guaranteed a right to legal aid, judicial review and to an oral hearing. The novelty is that such procedural rights don't necessarily have to be exercised inside the state in which a person is seeking asylum. An asylum seeker's rights, in other words, may be portable.

The portable-procedural approach seems less than ideal, yet it is an innovative theory that responds to the shortcomings of two alternative approaches. It avoids the problem of a German-style right to asylum, where enshrined constitutional rights lead to practical impossibilities. And it avoids the excessively punitive model for processing asylum claims currently in place in many liberal democratic states, where asylum seekers are effectively left without any legal rights. The application of a portable-procedural approach may well ensure significant improvements to offshore processing. It would at least guarantee that any offshore processing would involve humane treatment of asylum seekers. As stated in the Refugee Convention, asylum seekers shouldn't be penalised for the manner in which they have entered Australian territory. If we are to process asylum claims, there should be legislated minimum standards for the treatment of all asylum seekers in any offshore processing centre, ensuring adequate legal protections and respect for human rights.[41]

At the time of writing, the prospect of the Gillard government implementing its Malaysia Solution remains uncertain. There have been suggestions that the High Court's August 2011 judgement in the *Plaintiff M70* case has the effect of precluding not only a form of offshore processing in Malaysia but also any offshore processing in Nauru and Manus Island.[42] For the most part, the Gillard government has maintained its preference for a swap of asylum seekers with Malaysia – a policy which it believes will break the 'business model' of people smugglers. But it has also left open the possibility of abandoning this position, should that be the recommendation of an expert panel on asylum seeker policy led by retired Air Chief Marshal Angus Houston (appointed in June 2012 and due to offer its advice by August 2012). In theoretical terms, it is unclear whether a Malaysia Solution could be considered an exemplar of the portable-procedural approach. Given that Malaysia isn't a signatory to the Refugee Convention, asylum seekers sent there may not enjoy adequate conditions of protection.

Still, if we accept that public policy must operate in a non-ideal context, and further accept that moving towards a portable-procedural model has merit, something such as the Malaysia Solution could have some positive effects. As Menadue et al. argue:

> Viewed through a regional lens it can become a catalyst to start the process of building a durable protection system in the region and delivering protection dividends for all asylum seekers … Malaysia as a transit country is a key player in delivering a long term solution – indeed UNHCR in its recently released Global Report noted that while there are problems, 'constructive dialogue with national authorities has resulted in an improvement of the situation'. If this can be achieved we can dare to hope that – just as ASEAN is developing a regional Human Rights Instrument – we can look forward in the future to a Regional Protection Instrument.[43]

We shouldn't dismiss the importance of ensuring there is a regional focus: clearly, one country alone can't solve the world's refugee problem. We often forget that Asian neighbours such as Indonesia, Malaysia and Thailand receive a disproportionately large number of asylum seekers. It is important, therefore, to have some sharing of the burden in the region. If Australia can help promote a regional framework, that would remove incentives for dangerous boat journeys to be undertaken and possibly see a higher number of refugees resettled. This is arguably one of the few points on which all political parties could agree. To this end, it would be a demonstration of good faith for Australia to increase its intake of refugees under the humanitarian program from the current 13 750 in 2009–10 to something in the range of 25 000.[44] This increase would be based on a resettlement of refugees currently in countries such as Indonesia, Malaysia and Thailand. Such a stance would help contribute to a durable regional solution. Our regional neighbours are unlikely to engage in developing a credible regional response if they believe that Australia does not take its fair share of refugees. As things stand, our neighbours see Australian policy as simply a matter of 'burden shifting' rather than 'burden sharing' – that is, as something that works to their relative disadvantage.

There is one good precedent for regional cooperation on refugees. As highlighted earlier, when thousands of Indochinese refugees from south-east Asia were resettled in Australia, this was for the most part done through offshore processing, and conducted within a cooperative regional framework. That such refugees would go on to become proud citizens in a multicultural Australia, and make a positive contribution to Australian society, should remind us that we needn't fear that our generosity will be abused. We needn't fear the boats, or the people that come on them.

Afterword:
Having a go

A few years ago I was a guest on a radio program, having been invited to talk about Australian identity. After a brief discussion, the host took some calls from listeners. I vividly recall the contribution from a listener called Mick. 'When I think of Australia,' he said, 'I think of hardworking blokes and good-looking sheilas. I don't think anyone cares where you come from, as long as you have a go.' Some of us may rightly bristle at the ockerisms, but Mick gets the basic point correct. That ethos of having a go, and giving people a fair go, is about as authentically Australian as it gets.

When I pause to think of my own family's experience settling in Australia, I am reminded that we shouldn't take this for granted. Those who haven't made the journey of migration can underestimate the profundity of moving to another country. For the newly arrived immigrant, a small dose of generosity can often go a long way, and in ways you mightn't contemplate. My parents recall how in their initial years working in Sydney – they spoke only a basic level of English on arrival – they were helped by work colleagues who would stand next to them when they answered the phone, or take the time to explain unfamiliar terms. Almost three decades on, 'No worries' and 'How are you, mate?' are phrases they utter as naturally as they might say 'Khop chai' or 'Sabaidee' in Lao. Though they would still consider themselves Lao, or Chinese-Lao in the case of my father, they also take pride in being Australian in their particular way. They look back upon their decision to move here from France, and to become Australian citizens, without regret. Their story, my family's story, has very much been the one inscribed on that Freedom Gate in Cabramatta: 'To be renovative and integrate.'

For the most part, those who have come to this country as immigrants have enjoyed a fair go. During the past four decades, an official multiculturalism has recognised cultural diversity as a strength rather than a weakness of Australian society. As practised in Australia, the policy of multiculturalism has been about liberal citizenship. It has been about ensuring that all Australians can participate in the life of the nation without feeling that they have to discard their cultural heritage and identity. The model pursued by Australia has been a very different one to any so-called multiculturalism elsewhere in the world, particularly in Western Europe. When critics point to Europe's troubles with immigration and integration as a warning of what is to come here, they are simply drawing the wrong lessons. They commit a form of cultural cringe, failing to remember that on matters of diversity Australia has been an international exemplar.

Despite its success, multiculturalism has always been subject to some measure of public opposition. The first significant hostile voices came from Geoffrey Blainey and John Howard in the 1980s; in the 1990s, Pauline Hanson took resentment against multiculturalism to a new level of intensity. But it was as Prime Minister that Howard converted these sentiments into a nationalist populism which still features in Australian politics. There remain misgivings about multiculturalism. Quite apart from the Europe-inspired conservative critique, some continue to view it as a form of cultural relativism, or as implying that the only cultures worth celebrating are minority, 'ethnic' ones. For Australians who hold this view, there is little that could be said to persuade them of the merits of multiculturalism. Moreover, there are many others who, while accepting the benefits of a diverse society, nonetheless stop short of supporting official multiculturalism. Cultural diversity, they say, is something that should be dealt with organically: it should be a case of simply sitting back, allowing Australians of different ethnic and cultural origins to mix, and then watching a new 'race' of Australians emerge. Such processes do take place, and should be welcomed, but they take time. Rather than let integration take its own course, Australian governments since the 1970s have chosen a multicultural, nation-building posture. They have been right to do so.

Where to next, then, for multiculturalism? We shouldn't underestimate the importance of maintaining multicultural policy if Australia continues taking in a substantial number of immigrants each year. The settlement and integration of future immigrants would suffer if it were to be abandoned. At the same time, it shouldn't just be more of the same; there are some obvious areas for improvement. For example, there are still significant barriers to the recognition of newly arrived immigrants' skills and qualifications – many arrivals don't end up working in those areas that justified their original admission into the country, with an obvious impact on their ability to integrate. An increasing number of observers have also suggested that the provision of English tuition and assistance for those who arrive in Australia as refugees may need to be bolstered.[1] Clearly, the continued success of a multicultural Australia can't be divorced from the efficiency of the overall immigration program, and from the settlement services that we provide to new arrivals.

Whether there needs to be a new legislative focus for multicultural policy is more contentious. Namely, there have been calls from some quarters for the introduction of a *Commonwealth Multicultural Act*. This would enshrine multicultural principles in law in a manner similar to what has already been done in states including Victoria and New South Wales. According to its advocates, such legislation would provide a permanent benchmark against which multicultural policies could be measured. It could also include the creation of a federal statutory body on multicultural affairs, perhaps answerable to the Prime Minister and with its own budget. This would depart from the current arrangement, where multicultural policy at the Commonwealth level is subject to periodic renewal, and implemented by the Department of Immigration and Citizenship.

There are some sound reasons for supporting a *Multicultural Act* at the Commonwealth level, but little likelihood of any legislation of the kind being passed in the near future. The idea has already been rejected by senior figures in the Gillard Labor government, including Immigration Minister Chris Bowen; it has little support within the federal Coalition. In any case, a *Multicultural Act* shouldn't be regarded as a panacea. Its effectiveness would depend on the political context. Introducing a *Multicultural Act* would arguably achieve little if it weren't supported by both sides of politics; the establishment of a statutory multicultural body answering to the Prime Minister would, again, have limited significance if the sitting Prime Minister weren't an enthusiastic champion of multiculturalism. Indeed, the real challenge mightn't be so much about policy but about people and politics. The passing of a Commonwealth Act or the establishment of a new federal bureaucracy would arguably do little to persuade sceptics of the merits of multiculturalism. It is tempting for multicultural pragmatists to be content that the policy fight, to some extent, is now about conserving past gains. While a Commonwealth legislative framework would represent an advance, the failure to secure it would not be fatal. The architecture of multicultural policy is already securely in place, especially at the state level. That, perhaps, has been the great quiet victory of Australian multiculturalism.

But the battle in the realm of political culture is far from won. There is a need for a return to bipartisan political support for multiculturalism, for a start. Critics may disparage or belittle statements about cultural diversity as 'gesture politics', but the symbolism of politics matters. The language that politicians use, the manner in which they debate issues – these help set the *tone* of the national conversation. The past two decades have seen political leaders appeal to nationalist populism, at some cost to social harmony and public discourse. This is true of how they discuss not only matters directly relating to multiculturalism and immigration, but also related issues such as population growth and asylum seekers. What we must avoid, at all costs, is an escalation of rhetoric that can spur on political extremism and violence. The debate in Europe about Anders Breivik, a one-time member of the right-wing Norwegian Progress Party, whose murder of 77 people in Norway was committed in the cause of destroying multiculturalism, is one that merits our attention. That something such as the July 2011 attacks could happen in Norway, a bastion of tolerant Scandinavian social democracy, confirms that we shouldn't be indifferent to the possible dangers.

All this may simply reflect the historical evolution of the multicultural debate. Where once multiculturalism was more emphatically about securing rights, or about cultural maintenance, it is now about the *ethos* of how we negotiate diversity in Australian life. This question of ethos isn't confined to politicians. While notions of civic duty are typically invoked with respect to immigrants having to adhere to Australian values, they must also guide how all citizens respond to diversity. The test here is whether Australians are prepared to take their responsibilities as citizens seriously. If we do support a multicultural Australia, we must stand up for it when it matters. We must, for example, have the courage to confront racism when we see it in our everyday lives, at work, in our streets, or on buses or trains. Most fundamentally, we must recognise that multiculturalism isn't merely concerned with minorities and immigrants; it is about all Australians. It is about how we understand ourselves as a nation and as a people.

As this book went to press, the Gillard government's White Paper on 'Australia in the Asian Century', authored by former Treasury secretary Ken Henry, was yet to be published. But the ongoing debate about Australia's place in Asia prompted by the White Paper suggests there is a renewed importance to multiculturalism.

It is a point that mightn't be obvious at first. Much of our discussion about the region has been ruthlessly mercantilist. Almost without noticing it, we've fallen into the habit of making an economic fetish out of Australia's relationships with our Asian neighbours, seeing their value only in terms of dollar signs. The reflex is to talk about maximising the 'returns' from our 'investment' in Asia, or regarding our significant Asian immigrant population as a 'human resource' or 'asset'.[2] Yet, if Australia is truly to be part of an Asian century, something more than economic engagement is needed. We must be prepared to learn, culturally, from the dynamism and diverse traditions of the region. Might observing youthful democratic cultures help us understand our own democracy better? Might there be value in reflecting on the similarities between Asian concepts of communal obligation and our own value of mateship? To paraphrase Kipling, what should they know of Australia who only Australia know?[3]

Cultural learning of this sort isn't beyond our reach. Our multiculturalism provides a platform for extending our relations with the region. Yet an Asian century might also open the way for a new phase of Australian multiculturalism, one which seeks to transform the cultural literacy of future citizens. In the realm of language, multicultural policy has been focused on ensuring fluency in English for recent arrivals, but future policy may also need to include a concern with the teaching of foreign languages in Australian society.[4] The woeful state of enrolments in foreign languages in schools and universities is certainly something that must be rectified. But is it any wonder we struggle to get students in schools and universities to take up Asian languages when we can only speak of Asia as an economic entity rather than also a cultural one? We can't seriously expect to build Asian literacy while we treat it as a mere instrument of economic self-interest, a means of securing a lucrative job at the end of one's university degree. That isn't the way to motivate children to take on the challenge of learning Mandarin or Indonesian, and to persevere. If multiculturalism is indeed about citizenship, we may need to add a new dimension to its content: ensuring that Australian citizens are fit for an Asian century.

There is one final aspect to multiculturalism and engagement with Asia. We often think about what we can *get* from Asia without considering what we can *offer* to our neighbours in the region. It may surprise some to learn that living with diversity isn't just a challenge facing Western liberal democracies, but one facing many countries in Asia. Everywhere, people are grappling with the challenge of living peacefully amid differences. In his maiden speech to the Senate in February 2012, Foreign Affairs Minister Bob Carr laid down a particular challenge: 'We should ask what we Australians can do, in our modest way, to steer the world ... towards peaceful overlap and pluralism.'[5] In its own modest way, Australian multiculturalism can serve as a model of cultural diversity worth emulating, or at the very least from which others could learn. Many overseas regard our experience as a paragon of nation-building. Our society is diverse but cohesive. We have welcomed and absorbed successive waves of immigrants as citizens, all while preserving our easygoing, democratic culture. It is all evidence, you might say, of Australia's multicultural triumph – and reason for us to be confident and optimistic about its future.

Acknowledgments

My first thanks go to Pip McGuinness, for her unwavering confidence in this project from the outset. She has offered wise guidance and wonderful encouragement throughout. I can only hope the final result vindicates her support. I am also grateful to Uthpala Gunethilake for overseeing this book at NewSouth, and to Tricia Dearborn for her patience and judgement in editing the manuscript.

Gerald Ng, Nick Dyrenfurth, Keir Reeves, Peter Balint and Peter Hughes kindly read drafts of the book at various stages. This book has benefited from their suggestions and criticisms. At the School of Journalism, Australian and Indigenous Studies at Monash, Kirsty Marshall provided valuable research support in the early stages of preparing this book; her expert knowledge of *Neighbours* turned out to be a surprisingly pleasant bonus. I acknowledge the School's assistance in making it possible for Kirsty to contribute to the project. More generally, the School and the National Centre for Australian Studies have provided an auspicious environment in which to conduct research.

At the risk of omitting some names, I was fortunate to have had helpful discussions or exchanges with Dirk Anthony, Kate Bagnall, John Brumby, Nick Bryant, James Button, Miriam Cosic, Emma Dawson, Hass Dellal, Michael Ebeid, Richard Fidler, Geoff Gallop, Carmel Guerra, Duncan Ivison, Andrew Jakubowicz, James Jupp, Anthony Kitchener, Andrew Leigh, Race Mathews, Patrick McGorry, Bruce Meagher, John Menadue, Julian Morrow, Thang Ngo, Paul Power, Peter Shergold, Karina Sommers, Rauf Soulio, Joe Skrzynski, Helen Szoke, Lindsay Tanner, Andrew West and Carla Wilshire. I have learned much from my colleagues on the Australian Multicultural Council, and from my colleagues at Monash, particularly Bruce Scates, Rae Frances, Keir Reeves, Andrew Reeves – with whom I am working on an Australian Research Council Linkage Project, 'Anzac Day at Home and Abroad'.

Parts of this book draw upon work I have completed for Per Capita, particularly those concerning population policy. I thank David Hetherington, who has tolerated my extended absence from Per Capita while writing this book, and who has been a valued colleague and friend. In 2011, I was also a fellow at St James Ethics Centre, where I worked on the ethics of asylum and refugees: thank you to Simon Longstaff, Sally Treeby and Cris Parker for their support. Chapter 5 is based on the paper I prepared at the conclusion of my fellowship. Some aspects of this book's arguments have also been rehearsed in various columns in *The Age*. I am indebted to Paul Ramadge and Paul Austin for giving me a regular spot in the newspaper.

My final thanks go to my family. My parents Thinh and Chanthavone are living exemplars of multicultural integration, and are a permanent source of inspiration. My sister Sara is a fellow traveller in cultural diversity. I owe my greatest debt to Sarah Hepworth, who had to put up with a prolonged, punishing season of writing and editing in 2011 and 2012. I couldn't have asked for anyone more supportive. Her love is always a source of encouragement and her spirit a reminder of the better angels of our nature. I dedicate this book to her.

Notes

Introduction

1   John Rawls, *A Theory of Justice*, Harvard University Press,
      Cambridge, MA, 1971. For a fuller reading of Rawls's political
      philosophy, see also his *Political Liberalism*, Columbia University
      Press, New York, 1993.

2   James Jupp, 'Politics, Public Policy and Multiculturalism',
      in Michael Clyne and James Jupp (eds), *Multiculturalism and
      Integration: A Harmonious Relationship*, ANU E Press, Canberra,
      2011.

3   Francis Fukuyama, 'Identity, Immigration and Democracy',
      Journal of Democracy, Vol. 17, No. 2 (2006), p. 15.

4   Chris Bowen, 'The Genius of Australian Multiculturalism',
      Address to the Sydney Institute, Sydney, 17 February 2011,
      available at www.minister.immi.gov.au/media/cb/2011/
      cb159251.htm (last accessed 17 April 2012).

5   Geoffrey Brahm Levey, 'Multiculturalism and Terror', in
      Raimond Gaita (ed.), *Essays on Muslims and Multiculturalism*, Text
      Publishing, Melbourne, 2011, p. 21.

6   See, e.g., John Hirst, 'More or Less Diverse', in Helen Irving
      (ed.), *Unity and Diversity: A National Conversation. The Barton Lectures*,
      ABC Books, Sydney, 2001.

7   See John Howard, *Lazarus Rising: A Personal and Political
      Autobiography*, HarperCollins, Sydney, 2010, pp. 173–5.

8   W. B. Gallie, 'Essentially Contested Concepts', *Proceedings of the
      Aristotelian Society*, Vol. 56 (1956).

1   The life and times of multiculturalism

1   Donald Horne, *Time of Hope: Australia 1966–72*, Angus &
      Robertson, Sydney, 1980, p. 179.

2   Al Grassby, *A Multi-Cultural Society for the Future*, AGPS, Canberra,
      1973.

3   Grassby, *A Multi-Cultural Society for the Future*, p. 15.

4   Jean Martin, *The Migrant Presence: Australian Responses 1947–1977.
      Research Report for the National Population Inquiry*, Allen & Unwin,
      Sydney, 1978, p. 55.

5   Richard White, *Inventing Australia: Images and Identity 1688–1980*, Allen & Unwin, Sydney, 1981, p. 159.

6   Gwenda Tavan, *The Long, Slow Death of White Australia*, Scribe, Melbourne, 2005, p. 41.

7   Tavan, *The Long, Slow Death of White Australia*, p. 42.

8   James Jupp, *Arrivals and Departures*, Cheshire-Lansdowne, Melbourne, 1966, pp. 13–14.

9   Jupp, *Arrivals and Departures*. For a contrasting view, see Hirst, who offers a more sympathetic view of assimilation as merely a form of integration that insisted immigrants 'did not parade their differences or transfer their old-world disputes to this new land' rather than that 'they immediate drop their old ways': Hirst, 'More or Less Diverse', p. 115.

10   See Arthur Calwell, 'Two Wongs Do Not Make a White', in Sally Warhaft (ed.), *Well May We Say: The Speeches That Made Australia*, Black Inc., Melbourne, 2004, p. 246.

11   For an instructive history of the gradual dismantling of the White Australia policy, see Tavan, *The Long, Slow Death of White Australia*.

12   Martin, *The Migrant Presence*, p. 207.

13   Nino Culotta, *They're a Weird Mob: A Novel*, Ure Smith, Sydney, 1957, p. 200.

14   Ben Maddison, 'The Australian Legend, Russel Ward and the Parallel Universe of Nino Culotta', *Journal of Australian Colonial History*, Vol. 10, No. 2 (2008).

15   Culotta, *They're a Weird Mob*, p. 204. Cf. Russel Ward, *The Australian Legend*, Oxford University Press, Melbourne, 1958. As noted by Ben Maddison in 'The Australian Legend, Russel Ward and the Parallel Universe of Nino Culotta', there are obvious similarities between Culotta's description of the typical Australian and Ward's classic portrait of an Australian national character derived from the ethos of bush workers.

16   See Jupp, *Arrivals and Departures*; Martin, *The Migrant Presence*, pp. 30–31.

17   See Mark Lopez, *The Origins of Multiculturalism in Australian Politics 1945–1975*, Melbourne University Press, Melbourne, 2000, Ch. 3.

18   Cited in Freda Hawkins, *Critical Years in Immigration: Canada and Australia Compared*, UNSW Press, Sydney, 1989, pp. 219–20.

19   See Lopez, *The Origins of Multiculturalism in Australian Politics*, esp. Ch. 4.

20   Will Kymlicka, *Multicultural Odysseys: Navigating the New International Politics of Diversity*, Oxford University Press, Oxford, 2007, p. 91.

21   Grassby, *A Multi-Cultural Society for the Future*, pp. 10–11.

22 Martin, *The Migrant Presence*, p. 33.
23 Cited in Stephen Castles, Bill Cope, Mary Kalantzis, Michael Morrissey, *Mistaken Identity: Multiculturalism and the Demise of Nationalism in Australia*, Pluto Press, Sydney, 1988, p. 61.
24 Castles et al., *Mistaken Identity*, p. 59.
25 Gough Whitlam, *The Whitlam Government 1972–1975*, Viking, Ringwood, Vic, 1985, p. 501.
26 Martin, *The Migrant Presence*, p. 52.
27 Whitlam, *The Whitlam Government 1972–1975*, p. 506.
28 Tavan, *The Long, Slow Death of White Australia*, pp. 206–7. One criticism that can be made of the Whitlam era is that in 1974 it merged the Department of Immigration with the Department of Labour, a move somewhat dissonant with other developments.
29 See Nancy Viviani, *The Indochinese in Australia 1975–1995: From Burnt Boats to Barbecues*, Oxford University Press, Melbourne, 1996.
30 See Malcolm Fraser and Margaret Simons, *Malcolm Fraser: The Political Memoirs*, Melbourne University Press, Melbourne, 2010, p. 418
31 Fraser and Simons, *Malcolm Fraser: The Political Memoirs*, p. 421.
32 Fraser and Simons, *Malcolm Fraser: The Political Memoirs*, p. 427.
33 Commonwealth of Australia, *Migrant Services and Programs: Report of the Review of Post-arrival Programs and Services for Migrants* ('Galbally Report'), AGPS, Canberra, 1978, p. 104.
34 Fraser and Simons, *Malcolm Fraser: The Political Memoirs*, p. 435.
35 Andrew Theophanous, *Understanding Multiculturalism and Australian Identity*, Elikia Books, Melbourne, 1995, p. 28.
36 Theophanous, *Understanding Multiculturalism*, p. 51.
37 Mary Kalantzis, 'Immigration, Multiculturalism and Racism', in Susan Ryan and Troy Bramston (eds), *The Hawke Government: A Critical Retrospective*, Pluto Press, Sydney, 2003, p. 320.
38 Office of Multicultural Affairs, Department of Prime Minister and Cabinet, *National Agenda for a Multicultural Australia: Shaping Our Future*, AGPS, Canberra, 1989, pp. 53, vi.
39 Office of Multicultural Affairs, *National Agenda for a Multicultural Australia*, p. vii.
40 Kymlicka, *Multicultural Odysseys*, p. 83.
41 Castles et al, *Mistaken Identity*, p. 151.
42 Geoffrey Blainey, *All for Australia*, Methuen Heynes, Sydney, 1984, p. 132.
43 Blainey, *All for Australia*, pp. 158–60.
44 In Rex Collings (ed.), *Reflections of a Statesman: The Writings and Speeches of Enoch Powell*, Bellew, London, 1991, p. 390.
45 Committee to Advise on Australia's Immigration Policies, *Immigration: A Commitment to Australia* ('FitzGerald Report'), AGPS,

Canberra, 1988, p. 59. For a useful discussion of the politics behind the Fitzgerald Report and the response of the Office of Multicultural Affairs, see Andrew Jakubowicz, 'Playing the Triangle: Cosmopolitanism, Cultural Capital and Social Capital as Intersecting Scholarly Discourses about Social Inclusion and Marginalisation in Australian Public Policy Debates', *Cosmopolitan Civil Societies*, Vol. 3, No. 3 (2011), pp. 68–69.

46 Theophanous, *Understanding Multiculturalism*, p. 106.

47 Theophanous, *Understanding Multiculturalism*, p. 115.

48 Ross Garnaut, *Australia and the Northeast Asian Ascendency*, Report to the Prime Minister and the Minister for Foreign Affairs and Trade, AGPS, Canberra, 1989.

49 Office of Multicultural Affairs, Department of Prime Minister and Cabinet, *Productive Diversity in Business: Profiting from Australia's Multicultural Advantage*, AGPS, Canberra, 1990.

50 Office of Multicultural Affairs, *Productive Diversity in Business*, p. 4.

51 Paul Keating, 'The Benefits of Cultural Diversity', in Mark Ryan (ed.), *Advancing Australia: The Speeches of Paul Keating, Prime Minister*, Big Picture Publications, Sydney, 1995, p. 269.

52 Cited in Paul Kelly, *The March of Patriots: The Struggle for Modern Australia*, Melbourne University Press, Melbourne, 2009, p. 157.

53 Kelly, *The March of Patriots*, p. 151.

54 Pauline Hanson, First Speech to the House of Representatives, 10 September 1996, *Hansard*.

55 Pauline Hanson (compiled by George J. Merritt), *Pauline Hanson – The Truth: On Asian Immigration, the Aboriginal Question and the Future of Australia*, St George Publications, Parkholme, SA, 1997.

56 Michael Leach, 'Hansonism, Political Discourse and Australian Identity', in Michael Leach, Geoffrey Stokes and Ian Ward (eds), *The Rise and Fall of One Nation*, St Lucia, University of Queensland Press, 2000, p. 48.

57 Ian Ward, Michael Leach and Geoffrey Stokes, 'Introduction', in Ward et al. (eds), *The Rise and Fall of One Nation*, p. 9.

58 Leach, 'Hansonism, Political Discourse and Australian Identity', pp. 44ff.

59 Leach, 'Hansonism, Political Discourse and Australian Identity', pp. 50–51.

60 Isaiah Berlin, 'Nationalism', in Isaiah Berlin (Henry Hardy and Roger Hausheer, eds), *The Proper Study of Mankind: An Anthology of Essays*, Pimlico, London, 1998, p. 594.

61 Kelly, *The March of Patriots*, p. 286.

62 Dennis Shanahan, 'Most still enjoy a culture cocktail', *The Australian*, 22 December 2005, p. 1. Earlier in 2002, Howard even conceded that on multiculturalism he would have to 'go with the flow': see Mike Steketee, 'M-word is kosher again, but

politics won't let it prosper', *The Australian*, 9 May 2002, p. 12.

63   Australia, Department of Immigration and Multicultural
     Affairs, *A New Agenda for Multicultural Australia*, Department of
     Immigration and Multicultural Affairs, Canberra, 1999, pp. 6, 8.

64   Australia, Department of Immigration and Multicultural and
     Indigenous Affairs, *Multicultural Australia, United in Diversity:
     Updating the 1999 New Agenda for Multicultural Australia*, Department
     of Immigration and Multicultural and Indigenous Affairs,
     Canberra, 2003.

65   See Senate Standing Committee on Legal and Constitutional
     Affairs Estimates (Supplementary Budget Estimates), 30
     October 2006 (*Official Hansard*), pp. 192–4; and Senate
     Standing Committee on Legal and Constitutional Affairs
     Estimates (Budget Estimates), 22 May 2007 (*Official Hansard*),
     pp. 95–7. Available at www.aph.gov.au/Parliamentary_Business/
     Committees/Senate_Committees?url=legcon_ctte/index.htm
     (last accessed 24 April 2012).

66   See James Jupp, *How Well Does Australian Democracy Serve Immigrant
     Australians?*, Democratic Audit of Australia Report No. 1,
     Australian National University, Canberra, 2003, pp. 43–50.

67   James Curran, *The Power of Speech: Australian Prime Ministers Defining
     the National Image*, Melbourne University Press, Melbourne, p.
     241.

68   Curran, *The Power of Speech*, p. 264.

69   See Graeme Davison, 'Testing Times: Citizenship and "National
     Values" in Britain and Australia', in Gaita (ed.), *Essays on
     Muslims and Multiculturalism*. I also discuss citizenship testing in
     Tim Soutphommasane, *Reclaiming Patriotism: Nation-Building for
     Australian Progressives*, Cambridge University Press, Melbourne,
     2009; and *The Virtuous Citizen: Patriotism in a Multicultural Society*,
     Cambridge University Press, Cambridge, 2012.

70   Anne Davies and Stephanie Peatling, 'Australians racist? No
     way, says Howard', *Sydney Morning Herald*, 13 December 2005,
     p. 6.

71   See Ward, *The Australian Legend*.

72   See Judith Brett, 'Relaxed and Comfortable: The Liberal Party's
     Australia', *Quarterly Essay*, Vol. 19 (2005).

73   On the notion of 'packages', see Gregory Melleuish, *The
     Packaging of Australia: Politics and Culture Wars*, UNSW Press,
     Sydney, 1998.

74   Tony Abbott, 'The Coalition's Plan for More Secure Borders',
     Address to the Institute of Public Affairs, Melbourne, 27
     April 2012, available at www.tonyabbott.com.au/LatestNews/
     Speeches/tabid/88/articleType/ArticleView/articleId/8689/
     Address-to-the-Institute-of-Public-Affairs-Melbourne.aspx (last

accessed 30 April 2012).

75   Scott Morrison, 'Australia Day Statement: The Importance of Being Us', Media Release, 26 January 2011, available at www. scottmorrison.com.au/info/pressrelease.aspx?id=581 (last accessed 23 April 2012).

76   Lenore Taylor, 'Morrison sees votes in anti-Muslim strategy', *Sydney Morning Herald*, 17 February 2011, p. 1.

77   Patricia Karvelas, 'Hygiene lessons will help migrants integrate: Coalition', *The Australian*, 10 January 2012, p. 1.

2   The Australian model

1   Iris Marion Young, *Justice and the Politics of Difference*, Princeton University Press, Princeton, 1990; cf. Charles Taylor, 'The Politics of Recognition', in Amy Gutmann (ed.), *Multiculturalism: Examining the Politics of Recognition*, Princeton University Press, Princeton, 1994. For discussion of the limits of radical versions of a multicultural politics of difference, especially as it has been expressed in the American context, see Robert Hughes, *Culture of Complaint: The Fraying of America*, The Harvill Press, London, 1995 and Arthur Schlesinger, Jr, *The Disuniting of America: Reflections on a Multicultural Society*, W. W. Norton & Co., New York, 1992.

2   See Kymlicka, *Multicultural Odysseys*; Will Kymlicka, *Multicultural Citizenship: A Liberal Theory of Minority Rights*, Oxford University Press, Oxford, 1995.

3   Taylor, 'The Politics of Recognition', p. 38.

4   Tariq Modood, *Multiculturalism: A Civic Idea*, Polity, Cambridge, 2007, p. 8. For discussion of the relationship between liberalism and Australian multiculturalism, see the essays in Geoffrey Brahm Levey (ed.), *Political Theory and Australian Multiculturalism*, Berghan Books, New York, 2008.

5   For a philosophical discussion of public holidays and multiculturalism, see Geoffrey Brahm Levey, 'Symbolic Recognition, Multicultural Citizens, and Acknowledgement: Negotiating the Christmas Wars', *Australian Journal of Political Science*, Vol. 40, No. 4 (2006), pp. 355–70.

6   Government of Quebec, *The Consultation Commission on Accommodation Practices Related to Cultural Differences* ('Bouchard–Taylor Commission'), Final Report (Complete), Government of Quebec, Montreal.

7   Amartya Sen, *Identity and Violence: The Illusion and Destiny*, Allen Lane, London, 2006; Anne Phillips, *Multiculturalism Without Culture*, Princeton University Press, Princeton, 2007; Patchen Markell, *Bound by Recognition*, Princeton University Press, Princeton, 2003.

8   Pascal Bruckner, *The Tyranny of Guilt: An Essay on Western*

Masochism, Princeton University Press, Princeton, 2010, translated by Steven Rendall, p. 148

9   Modood, *Multiculturalism: A Civic Idea*, p. 105. See also Jock Collins, Carol Reid and Charlotte Fabiansson, 'Identities, Aspirations and Belonging of Cosmopolitan Youth in Australia', *Cosmopolitan Civil Societies Journal*, Vol. 3, No. 3 (2011), pp. 92–107.

10   Brian Galligan and Winsome Roberts, *Australian Citizenship*, Melbourne University Press, Melbourne, 2004.

11   Curran, *The Power of Speech*, pp. 237–8.

12   James Curran and Stuart Ward, *The Unknown Nation: Australia After Empire*, Melbourne University Press, Melbourne, 2010.

13   Benedict Anderson, *Imagined Communities: Reflections on the Origin and Spread of Nationalism*, Verso, London, 1991.

14   See Timothy Garton Ash, 'Germans, more or less', *New York Review of Books*, 24 February 2011, available at www.nybooks. com/articles/archives/2011/feb/24/germans-more-or-less/ (last accessed 23 April 2012).

15   David Cameron, Speech at Munich Security Conference, 5 February 2011, available at www.number10.gov.uk/news/pms-speech-at-munich-security-conference/ (last accessed 29 October 2011).

16   Gerard Henderson, 'Leaders are right to confront failures of multiculturalism', *Sydney Morning Herald*, 8 February 2011, p. 11.

17   Greg Sheridan, 'How I lost faith in multiculturalism', *Weekend Australian* (Inquirer), 2 April 2011, p. 1.

18   Janet Albrechtsen, 'Move over multiculturalism, your time is past', *The Australian*, 29 November 2006, p. 16.

19   Josh Gordon and Jewel Topsfield, 'Our values or go home: Costello', *The Age*, 24 February 2006, p. 1.

20   Peter Ryan, 'Apologise to Blainey', *The Australian*, 15 December 2005, p. 10.

21   For more detailed discussion of the Cronulla riots, see e.g. the contributions in Greg Noble (ed.), *Lines in the Sand: the Cronulla Riots, Multiculturalism and National Belonging*, Institute of Criminology, Sydney, 2009.

22   Keith Windschuttle, 'Howard, cultural warrior', *The Australian*, 21 February 2006, p. 14.

23   Paul Sheehan, 'A great divide', *Sydney Morning Herald*, 17 December 2005, p. 19.

24   Paul Sheehan, *Girls Like You: Four Young Girls, Six Brothers and a Cultural Timebomb*, PanMacmillan, Sydney, 2006. Sheehan has been a long-time critic of multiculturalism: see Paul Sheehan, *Among the Barbarians: The Dividing of Australia*, Random House, Sydney, 1998.

25   Ghassan Hage, 'Multiculturalism and the Ungovernable
       Muslim', in Gaita (ed.), *Muslims and Multiculturalism*.
26   Hage, 'Multiculturalism and the Ungovernable Muslim', p. 181.
27   In this respect, the critiques echo the arguments made by others
       in the European context: see e.g. Christopher Caldwell in his
       Reflections on the Revolution in Europe: Immigration, Islam and the West,
       Allen Lane, London, 2009.
28   Henderson, 'Leaders are right to confront failures of
       multiculturalism'.
29   Sheridan, 'How I lost faith in multiculturalism'.
30   For some discussions of Muslims and multiculturalism, see Gaita
       (ed.), *Essays on Muslims and Multiculturalism*.
31   Australian Bureau of Statistics, *Reflecting a Nation: Stories from
       the 2011 Census, 2012–2013*, Cat No. 2071.0, 2012, available at
       <www.abs.gov.au/ausstats/abs@.nsf/Lookup/2071.0main+featur
       es902012-2013> (last accessed 8 July 2012).
32   Henderson, 'Leaders are right to confront failures of
       multiculturalism'.
33   For an interesting recent discussion of multiculturalism in the
       context of French-speaking Canada, see the Bouchard–Taylor
       Commission. Among other things, Bouchard and Taylor discuss
       the notion of 'interculturalism'; cf. Geoffrey Brahm Levey,
       'Interculturalism vs Multiculturalism: A Distinction without a
       Difference?', *Journal of Intercultural Studies*, Vol. 33 (2012),
       pp. 217–24.
34   David Smith, Janice Wykes, Sanuki Jayarajah and Taya
       Fabijanic, 'Citizenship in Australia', Paper for OECD Seminar
       on Naturalisation and the Socio-Economic Integration of
       Immigrants and their Children, October 2010, Department of
       Immigration and Citizenship, Canberra, 2010, p. 9, available at
       www.immi.gov.au/media/publications/research/_pdf/citizenship-
       in-australia-2011.pdf (last accessed 23 April 2012).
35   See 'Chen, Kim, Singh are the new big names', *Sydney Morning
       Herald* (online), 25 January 2012, available at www.smh.com.
       au/national/chen-kim-singh-are-the-new-big-names-20120124-
       1qffe.html (last accessed 25 January 2012).
36   Val Colic-Peisker, '"Ethnics" and "Anglos" in the Labour Force:
       Advancing Australia Fair?', *Journal of Intercultural Studies*, Vol. 32,
       No. 6 (2011), pp. 637–54.
37   Thomas Liebig and Sarah Widmaier, 'Children of Immigrants in
       the Labour Markets of EU and OECD Countries: An Overview',
       OECD, Paris, 2009, pp. 17, 23.
38   Jeevan Vasagar, 'Black student intake at Oxford University rises
       to 32', *Guardian* (online), 18 December 2011, available at www.
       guardian.co.uk/education/2011/dec/18/black-students-oxford-

university-rises (last accessed 19 March 2012).

39   See Caspar Floris van den Berg, *Transforming for Europe: The Reshaping of National Bureaucracies in a System*, Leiden University Press, Leiden, 2011.

40   Oliver Marc Hartwich, *Selection, Migration and Integration: Why Multiculturalism Works in Australia (and Fails in Europe)*, Centre for Independent Studies, Sydney, 2011.

41   See Stephen Castles, 'Multicultural Citizenship: A Response to the Dilemma of Globalisation and National Identity?', Journal of Intercultural Studies, Vol. 18, No. 1 (1997), pp. 5–22.

42   Hartwich, *Selection, Migration and Integration*, p. 6; see also OECD, *Jobs for Immigrants, Vol. 1 – Labour Market Integration in Australia, Denmark and Sweden*, OECD, Paris, 2007, Ch. 4.

43   See Cecile Laborde, *Critical Republicanism: The Hijab Controversy and Political Philosophy*, Oxford University Press, Oxford, 2008.

44   Paul Scheffer, *Immigration Nations* (Liz Waters, trans.), Polity, Cambridge, 2011.

45   Scheffer, *Immigration Nations*, p. 114.

46   Modood, *Multiculturalism: A Civic Idea*, p. 33.

47   Commission on the Future of Multi-Ethnic Britain, *The Future of Multi-Ethnic Britain* ('Parekh Report'), Profile Books, London, 2000.

48   Sen, *Identity and Violence*.

49   See e.g. Suvendrini Perera, 'From "Sovereignty" to "Sustainability": The Loops and Lineaments of Exclusion 2001–2010', in Suvendrini Perera, Graham Seal and Sue Summers (eds), *Enter at Own Risk? Australia's Population Questions for the 21st Century*, Black Swan Press, Perth, 2010.

3   How racist is this country?

1   See Mungo MacCallum, *Australian Story: Kevin Rudd and the Lucky Country*, Quarterly Essay No. 36, Black Inc, Melbourne, 2009, p. 64.

2   For more detailed discussion of patriotism, see Soutphommasane, *Reclaiming Patriotism* and *The Virtuous Citizen*.

3   Some, however, draw a distinction between the Australian public's acceptance of 'soft multiculturalism' as opposed to 'hard multiculturalism', mirroring my point about multiculturalism in its descriptive sense and in its policy one: see Andrew Markus, 'Attitudes to Multiculturalism and Cultural Diversity'.

4   A 2010 study by Ipsos based on a nationally representative sample of 1081 showed that 62 per cent of respondents either agree or strongly agree that 'Australia should be a multicultural society', and that 61 per cent agree or strongly agree that 'Immigrants have enriched the Australian way of life'. Such a

finding is corroborated by the Scanlon Foundation's regular *Mapping Social Cohesion* reports, which in four surveys since 2007 has found that between 62.4 and 67.9 per cent of its respondents (N = at least 2000) agree or strongly agree with the statement 'Accepting immigrants from many different countries makes Australia stronger'. See Ipsos Australia, *SBS Immigration Nation Thought Leadership Research Final Report*, Ipsos, Sydney 2010, p. 14; Andrew Markus, *Mapping Social Cohesion: The Scanlon Foundation Surveys (Summary Report) 2011*, Monash University, Melbourne, 2011, p. 18.

5   Charlie Teo, Australia Day 2012 Address, New South Wales Conservatorium of Music, Sydney, 23 January 2012, available at www.australiaday.com.au/whatson/australiadayaddress2.aspx?AddressID=30 (last accessed 19 April 2012).

6   Ipsos's survey in 2010 found that 13 per cent of respondents reported experiencing discrimination, while the Scanlon Foundation survey of 2011 found that 14 per cent of its respondents reported it (compared to 9 per cent in 2007, 10 per cent in 2009 and 14 per cent in 2010): see Ipsos, *SBS Immigration Nation Thought Leadership Research Final Report*, p. 15; Markus, *Mapping Social Cohesion*, p. 17.

7   Jon Stratton, *Race Daze: Australia in Identity Crisis*, Pluto Press, Sydney, 1998; Ghassan Hage, *White Nation: Fantasies of White Supremacy in a Multicultural Society*, Pluto Press, Sydney, 2000.

8   I adopt this point from BBC correspondent Nick Bryant, who offers an illuminating perspective on Australian racism and how it compares with American and British racism: see Nick Bryant, *Adventures in Correspondentland*, William Heinemann, Sydney, 2011, pp. 370–5.

9   Liz Jackson, ABC TV, 'Riot and revenge', *Four Corners*, 13 March 2006, transcript available at www.abc.net.au/4corners/content/2006/s1590953.htm (last accessed 29 April 2012). For commentary on the Cronulla riots, see the essays in Gregory Noble (ed.), *Lines in the Sand: The Cronulla Riots, Multiculturalism and National Belonging*, Institute of Criminology Press, Sydney, 2009.

10   ABC TV, 'Front page – Jones and Cronulla', *Media Watch*, Episode 2, 20 February 2006, transcript available at www.abc.net.au/mediawatch/transcripts/s1574155.htm (last accessed 29 April 2012).

11   Malcolm Knox, 'Comment: Cronulla Five Years On', *The Monthly*, December 2010–January 2011.

12   Perera, 'From "Sovereignty" to "Sustainability"', pp. 1–2.

13   Stephen Castles, 'The Racisms of Globalisation', in Ellie Vasta and Stephen Castles (eds), *The Teeth are Smiling: The Persistence of Racism in Multicultural Australia*, Allen & Unwin, Sydney, 1996,

pp. 17–45.

14 Stratton, *Race Daze*, p. 11.

15 Modood, *Multiculturalism: A Civic Idea*, p. 45.

16 House of Representatives Joint Standing Committee on Migration Inquiry into Multiculturalism in Australia ('Inquiry into Multiculturalism'), 2011–12: see www.aph.gov.au/Parliamentary_Business/Committees/House_of_Representatives_Committees?url=mig/multiculturalism/index.htm (last accessed 23 April 2012).

17 Name withheld, Submission No. 30, Inquiry into Multiculturalism.

18 Name withheld, Submission No. 200, Inquiry into Multiculturalism.

19 'B M', Submission No. 195, Inquiry into Multiculturalism.

20 See, e.g., Arjun Ramachandran, 'Harris Park violence going on for years', *Sydney Morning Herald* (online), 10 June 2009, available at www.smh.com.au/national/harris-park-violence-going-on-for-years-20090610-c2z0.html (last accessed 24 April 2012); Bonnie Malkin, 'Indian students stage violent protest over attacks in Australia', *Daily Telegraph* (London) (online), 9 June 2009, available at www.telegraph.co.uk/news/worldnews/australiaandthepacific/australia/5486102/Indian-students-stage-violent-protest-over-attacks-in-Australia.html (last accessed 5 April 2012).

21 A. G. Greenwald, B. A. Nosek and M. R. Banaji, 'Understanding and Using the Implicit Association Test', *Journal of Personality and Social Psychology*, Vol. 85 (2003), pp. 197–216.

22 Taylor, 'The Politics of Recognition', p. 25.

23 For scientific studies demonstrating this connection, see Vic Health, *Making the Link between Cultural Discrimination and Health*, Vic Health Letter, 1 June 2007, available at www.vichealth.vic.gov.au/en/Publications/VicHealth-Letter/Making-the-link-between-cultural-discrimination-and-health.aspx (last accessed 5 April 2012); Vic Health, *Ethnic and Race-Based Discrimination as a Determinant of Mental Health and Wellbeing*, Research Summary 3, 2008, available at www.vichealth.vic.gov.au/en/Publications/Freedom-from-discrimination/Ethnic-and-race-based-discrimination-as-a-determinant-of-mental-health-and-wellbeing.aspx (last accessed 4 June 2012).

24 Hage, 'Multiculturalism and the Ungovernable Muslim', pp. 34–5.

25 Australian Federation of Islamic Councils, 'Multiculturalism and the Australian Muslim Community', Submission No. 341, Inquiry into Multiculturalism.

26 Brian Barry, *Culture and Equality: An Egalitarian Critique of*

Multiculturalism, Polity, Cambridge, 2001, p. 252.

27 One possible current exception concerns the recognition of Aboriginal customary law in some remote Indigenous communities.

28 Taylor, 'The Politics of Recognition', p. 68.

29 Taylor, 'The Politics of Recognition', pp. 67, 73.

30 See Duncan Ivison, 'The Moralism of Multiculturalism', *Journal of Applied Philosophy*, Vol. 22, No. 2 (2005), pp. 169–82. In recent years, some political theorists have advanced the idea of 'interculturalism' to describe the political culture demanded. Arguably, any difference between this and the multiculturalism I have outlined here would be merely semantic.

31 Andrew Bolt, 'Silencing me impedes unity', *Herald Sun*, 29 September 2011, p. 1.

32 *Eatock v Bolt* [2011] FCA 1103.

33 See Bhikhu Parekh, *Rethinking Multiculturalism: Cultural Diversity and Political Theory*, 2nd ed., Palgrave Macmillan, Basingstoke, 2005.

34 Ann Black and Kerrie Sadiq, 'Good and Bad Sharia: Australia's Mixed Response to Islamic Law', *UNSW Law Journal*, Vol. 17, No. 1 (2011), pp. 82–99.

35 This doesn't mean that we must reject every cultural practice pursued under sharia – where a cultural practice is consistent with existing Australian law, there is no problem.

36 See Amy Gutmann and Dennis Thompson, *Democracy and Disagreement: Why Moral Conflict Cannot Be Avoided in Politics, and What Should Be Done About It*, Harvard University Press, Cambridge MA, 1996. For a detailed discussion of the relationship between citizenship, national culture and deliberative democracy, see Soutphommasane, *The Virtuous Citizen*.

37 Guy Rundle, 'Friday Book Review: *Reclaiming Patriotism*', *Crikey*, 20 November 2009, available at www.crikey.com.au/2009/11/20/rundles-friday-book-review-reclaiming-patriotism/ (last accessed 6 April 2012). For my response, see Tim Soutphommasane, 'Dear Guy Rundle: being an immigrant doesn't disqualify me from debating Aussie identity', *Crikey*, 23 November 2009, available at www.crikey.com.au/2009/11/23/dear-guy-rundle-being-an-immigrant-doesn%E2%80%99t-disqualify-me-from-debating-aussie-identity/ (last accessed 6 April 2012).

38 For an example of this line of argument, see Nikki Gemmell, *Why You Are Australian: A Letter to My Children*, Harper Collins, Sydney, 2009.

39 David Miller, *On Nationality*, Oxford University Press, Oxford, 1995, p. 158.

40 Admittedly, the dividing line between social norms and 'national

character' is a difficult one to delineate. But, philosophically, a public culture isn't a mere extension of a private culture: see Soutphommasane, *Reclaiming Patriotism*, pp. 46–52.

41 Miriam Dixson, *The Imaginary Australian: Anglo-Celts and Identity*, UNSW Press, Sydney, 1999; Galligan and Roberts, *Australian Citizenship*.

42 Hirst, 'More or Less Diverse', p. 117.

43 Colmar Brunton, *'A Century of Service': Community Research*, Colmar Brunton Social Research, Canberra, 2010, p. 5, available at www.anzaccentenary.gov.au/subs/2010/reports/researchreport.pdf (last accessed 6 April 2012).

44 See Marilyn Lake and Henry Reynolds, *What's Wrong with Anzac? The Militarisation of Australian History*, NewSouth Publishing, Sydney, 2010.

45 Gemma Jones and Nathan Mawby, 'Anzac fury: Gallipoli anniversary could divide nation, government report warns', *Herald Sun*, 26 March 2012, p. 1.

46 Kate Bagnall, 'That famous fighting family', *Inside History*, Vol. 9, 2012, pp. 37–40.

47 Alastair Davidson, 'Multiculturalism and citizenship: silencing the migrant voice, *Journal of Intercultural Studies*, Vol. 18, No. 2 (1997), p. 77.

48 Karina Anthony, *The Political Representation of Ethnic and Racial Minorities*, Briefing Paper No. 03/2006, New South Wales Parliamentary Library, Sydney, 2006. Anthony found that 12 per cent of the total of Australian state and Commonwealth parliamentarians could be classed as being from an 'ethnic minority' background; of those in the Commonwealth parliament, the total was 10 per cent.

49 Australian Bureau of Statistics, *Migration, Australia, 2009–10*. Cat. No. 3412.0, 2011, available at www.abs.gov.au/ausstats/abs@.nsf/Products/1197BC920F1A28E5CA2578B00011976A?opendocument#footnote1back (last accessed 6 April 2012).

50 Jupp, *How Well Does Australian Democracy Serve Immigrant Australians?*, p. 35.

51 The best discussion of ethnic politics and clientelist subcultures in Australian politics remains that in Gianni Zappala, *Four Weddings, a Funeral and a Family Reunion: Ethnicity and Representation in Australian Federal Politics*, AGPS, Canberra, 1997; see also Jen Tsen Kwok, 'Clientelism in the Ethnopolis: Ethnic Contribution Networks and Political Fundraising under Late Multiculturalism', *Journal of Australian Studies*, Vol. 32, No. 4 (2008), pp. 467–479.

52 Past and present Asian-Australian federal parliamentarians number fewer than half a dozen: Penny Wong (2002–present), Lisa Singh (Senate, 2010–present), Michael Johnson (House of

Representatives, 2001–10), Tsebin Tchen (Senate, 1999–2005), Bill O'Chee (Senate, 1990–99). Some consider Australia's first Asian elected federal representative to be Thomas Bakhap, Senator for Tasmania (Liberal, 1913–23), who had an adoptive Chinese father and an Irish-Australian mother. It is unclear whether Bakhap has any Chinese ethnicity but he nonetheless identified as Chinese-Australian.

53   This has included Helen Sham-Ho, Henry Tsang and Peter Wong in the NSW upper house, Hong Lim in the Victorian lower house, and Michael Choi in the Queensland legislature. Of this list, only Lim currently sits in parliament. Previous Asian-Australian lord mayors include John So in Melbourne and Robert Ho in Sydney.

54   Australian Public Service Commission, *State of the Service 2010–11*, Australian Public Service Commission, Canberra, Ch. 7, available at www.apsc.gov.au/publications-and-media/parliamentary-reports/state-of-the-service/state-of-the-service-2010/chapter-7-diversity (last accessed 30 May 2012).

55   Australian Public Service Commission, *State of the Service 2010–11*.

56   Department of Defence, *Department of Defence Census 2007: Public Report*, Department of Defence, Canberra, 2009, p. 7.

57   See report by Hayden Cooper and Nikki Tugwell, 'Facebook group reveals ugly side of Defence Force culture', ABC TV, 7.30, 29 February 2012, transcript available at www.abc.net.au/7.30/content/2012/s3442781.htm (last accessed 6 April 2012)

58   See report by Michael Edwards, 'Army chief calls for greater diversity', ABC Radio National, *AM*, 29 February 2012, transcript available at www.abc.net.au/am/content/2012/s3441934.htm (last accessed 6 April 2012).

59   I do not examine racism in sport in any great detail in this chapter, primarily because of length constraints. This isn't to deny the importance of the issue in that arena, particularly given the regularity with which racist controversies erupt in sport, and the powerful role of sport in Australia society.

60   Department of Immigration and Citizenship, 'Introduction of New Points Test', Department of Immigration and Citizenship, Canberra, 2010, available at www.immi.gov.au/skilled/general-skilled-migration/pdf/points-fact.pdf (last accessed 27 December 2011).

61   Department of Immigration and Citizenship, *Migrant Economic Outcomes and Contributions – April 2011*, Department of Immigration and Citizenship, Canberra, 2011, p. 4, available at www.immi.gov.au/media/publications/research/_pdf/outcomes-contributions-apr11.pdf (last accessed 6 April 2012).

62   Department of Immigration and Citizenship, *Migrant Economic*

Outcomes and Contributions – April 2011, p. 649.

63 Department of Immigration and Citizenship, *Migrant Economic Outcomes and Contributions – April 2011*, p. 638.

64 Alison Booth, Andrew Leigh and Elena Varganova, 'Does Racial and Ethnic Discrimination Vary Across Minority Groups? Evidence from a Field Experiment' (July 2010), CEPR Discussion Paper No. DP7913, available at SSRN: http://ssrn.com/abstract=1640989 (last accessed 6 April 2012).

65 Georgia Wilkins, 'Star hits out at Home and Away racism', *Sydney Morning Herald* (online), 16 February 2012, available at www.smh.com.au/entertainment/tv-and-radio/star-hits-out-at-home-and-away-racism-20120216-1ta23.html#ixzz1nsFoaqyl (last accessed 6 April 2012).

66 Grassby, *A Multi-Cultural Society for the Future*, p. 4.

67 Daniel Burt, 'Is Australian television racist?', *The Age* (Green Guide), 1 March 2012, p. 11, available at www.theage.com.au/entertainment/tv-and-radio/is-australian-television-racist-20120229-1u1jm.html#ixzz1nsV1U4lZ (last accessed 6 April 2012).

68 ABC TV, 'TT's false facts fuel fear', *Media Watch*, Episode 37, 24 October 2011, transcript available at www.abc.net.au/mediawatch/transcripts/s3346987.htm (last accessed 6 April 2012).

69 Nine Network, 'Asian Bride Invasion', *A Current Affair*, 26 April 2012; ABC TV, 'ACA's Culture Shock', *Media Watch*, Episode 13, 28 May 2007, transcript available at www.abc.net.au/mediawatch/transcripts/s1935713.htm (last accessed 6 April 2012).

70 Seven Network, 'Fake Identities', *Today Tonight*, 21 May 2012.

71 SBS Charter, available at www.sbs.com.au/aboutus/corporate/index/id/25/h/SBS-Charter (last accessed 24 April 2012).

72 Ien Ang, Gay Hawkins and Lamia Dabboussy, *The SBS Story: The Challenge of Diversity*, UNSW Press, Sydney, 2008, p. 6.

73 Ang, Hawkins and Dabboussy, *The SBS Story*, pp. 20–21.

74 Ang, Hawkins and Dabboussy, *The SBS Story*, p. 20.

75 See Will Kymlicka, *Contemporary Political Philosophy: An Introduction*, Oxford University Press, Oxford, 2002, Ch. 8; Robert E. Goodin, 'Liberal Multiculturalism: Protective and Polyglot', *Political Theory*, Vol. 34, No. 3 (2006), pp. 289–303.

4   A bigger Australia

1 Julia Gillard, 'Moving Australia Forward', Speech to the Lowy Institute for International Policy, Sydney, 6 July 2010, available at www.pm.gov.au/press-office/moving-australia-forward (last accessed 6 April 2012).

2 Gillard, 'Moving Australia Forward'.

3   Dick Smith, *Dick Smith's Population Crisis: The Dangers of Unsustainable Growth for Australia*, Allen & Unwin, Sydney, 2011.

4   In House of Representatives Standing Committee on Long Term Strategies ('Jones Report'), *Australia's Population "Carrying Capacity": One Nation – Two Ecologies*, AGPS, Canberra, 1994, p. 7.

5   In Geoffrey Blainey, *The Land Is All Horizons: Australian Fears and Visions*, Boyer Lectures 2001, ABC Books, Sydney, 2001, p. 5.

6   Stuart Macintyre, *A Concise History of Australia*, 2nd ed., Cambridge University Press, Cambridge, 2004, p. 170.

7   Paul Ehrlich, *The Population Bomb*, Ballantine Books, New York, 1968.

8   See National Population Council, *Population Issues and Australia's Future: Environment, Economy and Society*, AGPS, Canberra, 1992.

9   Jones Report, p. 125.

10 Jones Report,, p. 121. The report stopped short, however, of offering a clear recommendation of what numerical target should be adopted, preferring instead to canvass a number of possible options.

11 Department of Immigration and Citizenship, *The Outlook for Net Overseas Migration – December 2011*, Department of Immigration and Citizenship, Canberra, 2011, p. 3. In 2006 the Australian Bureau of Statistics changed its definition of who counts as an immigrant. Prior to 2006 the vast majority of those who arrived in Australia temporarily weren't counted in net overseas migration figures. Since then, people who enter Australia on a long-term temporary basis have been included.

12 Department of the Treasury, *Australia to 2050 – Future Challenges* ('Intergenerational Report'), Department of the Treasury, Canberra, 2010.

13 Department of the Treasury, Intergenerational Report.

14 Sustainable Development Panel, *Sustainable Development Panel Report: An Appendix to A Sustainable Population for Australia Issues Paper*, Department for Sustainability, Environment, Water, Population and Communities, Canberra, 2010.

15 Productivity Commission, *Economic Impacts of Migration and Population Growth*, Productivity Commission, Canberra, 2006.

16 Department of the Treasury, Intergenerational Report. For some useful commentary on the Intergenerational Report's analysis, see Prosperity and Productivity Panel, *Setting Up Australia for the Future: Report of the Productivity and Prosperity Advisory Panel*, Department for Sustainability, Environment, Water, Population and Communities, Canberra, 2010.

17 Allan Fels, 'Understanding How Population Affects the Quality of Competition in Our Economy', in Steve Vizard, Hugh J. Martin and Tim Watts (eds), *Australia's Population Challenge: The*

2002 *Australian Population Summit*, Penguin, Melbourne, 2003,
p. 45.

18   Phillipe Legrain, *Immigrants: Your Country Needs Them*, Little,
Brown, London, 2007, Ch. 4; Adrian Wooldridge, 'The battle
for brainpower', *Economist*, 5 October 2006, available at www.
economist.com/node/7961894?story_id=7961894 (last accessed
6 April 2012).

19   Legrain, *Immigrants: Your Country Needs Them*, p. 96.

20   Sam Lipski, 'Immigration Policy and the Global Search for
Scientific Talent', p. 29.

21   Ian Lowe, *Bigger or Better? Australia's Population Debate*, University of
Queensland Press, St Lucia, 2012, p. 117.

22   Jones Report, p. 143.

23   For a leading statement of the 'prosperity without growth' view,
see Tim Jackson, *Prosperity Without Growth: Economics for a Finite
Planet*, Earthscan, London, 2009.

24   Sustainable Development Panel, *Sustainable Development Panel
Report*, p. 29.

25   Lowe, *Bigger or Better?*, p. 185.

26   Lowe, *Bigger or Better?*, p. 27.

27   Lowe, *Bigger or Better?*, pp. 188–89.

28   George Megalogenis, 'A sustainable idea for marginals', *The
Australian*, 19 July 2010, p. 5.

29   See Hage, *White Nation*, Ch. 6, for discussion of another group,
Australians for an Ecologically Sustainable Population.

30   Ben Cubby, 'Anti-immigrants with a green tinge', *Sydney Morning
Herald* (online), 21 March 2003, available at www.smh.com.au/
articles/2003/03/21/1047749937122.html (last accessed 12 April
2012).

31   Lowe, *Bigger or Better?*, p. 169.

32   Rebecca Huntley and Bernard Salt, *Future Focus*, Ipsos Australia
and KPMG, 2010, p. 27, available at www.bernardsalt.com.
au/advisory/reports (last accessed 6 April 2012); see also Tim
Soutphommasane, *What Crisis? Wellbeing and the Australian Quality
of Life*, Per Capita, Sydney, 2011, available at www.percapita.org.
au/01_cms/details.asp?ID=331 (last accessed 30 April 2012).

33   Julia Gillard, Address to the Western Sydney Regional
Organisation of Councils National Population Summit, Casula,
NSW, 20 July 2010, available at www.alp.org.au/federal-
government/news/speech--address-to-the-western-sydney-
regional-org/ (last accessed 24 April 2012).

34   Bryant, *Adventures in Correspondentland*, p. 385.

35   See Joel Kotkin, *The Next Hundred Million: America in 2050*.
Penguin, New York, 2010; Edward Glaeser, *Triumph of the City*,
Penguin, New York, 2011.

36   Mercer, *Worldwide Quality of Living Survey 2011*, available at www.
      mercer.com/articles/quality-of-living-survey-report-2011 (last
      accessed 15 April 2012).

37   In 2011, Melbourne would dislodge Vancouver as the EIU's
      most liveable city. See Economist Intelligence Unit, *Global
      Liveability Report 2011*, available at www.eiu.com/site_info.
      asp?info_name=The_Global_Liveability_Report&rf=0 (last
      accessed 15 April 2012).

38   Department of the Treasury, Intergenerational Report.

39   Commsec, 'Australian homes are biggest in the world', *Commsec
      Economics*, 30 November 2009; see also Tim Soutphommasane,
      Just Get Over It: The Cost of Living in Australia, Per Capita, Sydney,
      2011, available at www.percapita.org.au/01_cms/details.
      asp?ID=420 (last accessed 30 May 2012).

40   Peter McDonald and Jeremy Temple, *Immigrants, Labour Supply and
      Per Capital Gross Domestic Product: Australia 2010–2050*, Department
      of Immigration and Citizenship, Canberra, 2010, p. 32.

41   Markus, *Mapping Social Cohesion*, pp. 23ff; cf. Ian McAllister, *The
      Australian Voter: 50 Years of Change*, UNSW Press, Sydney, 2011,
      Ch. 8.

42   See Peter Mares, 'Temporary Migration and Multiculturalism
      in Australia', Senate Occasional Lecture, 23 September 2011,
      available at www.aph.gov.au/About_Parliament/Senate/
      Research_and_Education/pops/pop57/c03 (last accessed 29
      April 2012); Peter McDonald and Jeremy Temple, *Immigration,
      Labour Supply and Per Capita Gross Domestic Product: Australia 2010–
      2050*, Department of Immigration and Citizenship, Canberra,
      2010, p. 12.

43   Department of Immigration and Citizenship, *Trends in Migration:
      Australia 2010–11*, Department of Immigration and Citizenship,
      Canberra, 2011.

44   Peter Mares, 'The Permanent Shift to Temporary Migration', in
      Perera et al. (eds), *Enter at Own Risk?*, pp. 66–67.

45   Michael Knight, *Strategic Review of the Student Visa Program 2011*,
      Department of Immigration and Citizenship, Canberra, 2011,
      available at www.immi.gov.au/students/knight (last accessed
      26 April 2012).

46   See Barbara Deegan, *Visa Subclass 457 Integrity Review Final Report*,
      Department of Immigration and Citizenship, Canberra, 2008,
      available at www.immi.gov.au/skilled/skilled-workers/_pdf/457-
      integrity-review.pdf (last accessed 30 May 2012).

47   See Rebecca Lawson, 'Gina's poetic swipe at critics', *Sunday
      Times* (Perth), 11 February 2012, available at www.perthnow.
      com.au/business/ginas-poetic-swipe-at-critics/story-
      e6frg2qc-1226268575661 (last accessed 27 April 2012).

48   ABC, 'Cameron "gobsmacked" at guest worker plan for WA',
     Radio National, *AM*, 26 May 2012, transcript available at www.
     abc.net.au/am/content/2012/s3511647.htm (last accessed 30
     May 2012); Kelvin Thomson, 'The problem with Enterprise
     Migration Agreements', *The Age* (online), 29 May 2012, www.
     theage.com.au/opinion/politics/the-problem-with-enterprise-
     migration-agreements-20120529-1zg1v.html#ixzz1wJQEtGee
     (last accessed 30 May 2012); Joo-Cheong Tham, '457 reasons
     for reform', *The Age*, 29 May 2012, p. 9.
49   Michael Walzer, *Spheres of Justice: A Defense of Pluralism and Equality*,
     Basic Books, New York, 1983, p. 61.

5 The sovereignty of fear

1   Nam Le, *The Boat*, Penguin, Melbourne, 2008, pp. 310–13.
2   Hieu Van Le, Annual Address on Immigration and Citizenship,
     Canberra, 16 June 2011, available at www.immi.gov.au/about/
     speeches-pres/_pdf/2011/2011-06-16-mr-hieu-van-le-ao.pdf
     (last accessed 7 April 2012).
3   See Peter Mares, *Borderline: Australia's Response to Refugees and Asylum
     Seekers*, UNSW Press, Sydney, 2001.
4   Megalogenis, *The Australian Moment*, p. 306. For other
     illuminating treatments of the politics of *Tampa*, see Kelly,
     The March of Patriots; David Marr and Marian Wilkinson, *Dark
     Victory*, Allen & Unwin, Sydney, 2003; Robert Manne, *Making
     Trouble: Essays Against the New Australian Complacency*, Black Inc.,
     Melbourne, 2011.
5   See e.g. Jessica Marszalek and Simon Benson, 'Boat people
     in our 'burbs: Floodgates open', *Herald Sun*, 26 November
     2011; Piers Akerman, 'Powerless to stop an invasion of boat
     people', *Daily Telegraph*, 16 September 2010, available at http://
     blogs.news.com.au/dailytelegraph/piersakerman/index.php/
     dailytelegraph/comments/powerless_to_stop_an_invasion_of_
     boat_people/ (last accessed 24 April 2012).
6   Tony Abbott, 'The Australian peaceful asylum invasion', *Daily
     Telegraph*, 15 December 2009, available at http://blogs.news.com.
     au/dailytelegraph/yoursay/index.php/dailytelegraph/comments/
     the_australian_peaceful_asylum_invasion/ (last accessed 24
     April 2012).
7   Legrain, *Immigrants: Your Country Needs Them*, p. 35.
8   Department of Immigration and Citizenship, *The Outlook for Net
     Overseas Migration – December 2011*, Department of Immigration
     and Citizenship, Canberra, 2011, p. 9; Department of
     Immigration and Citizenship, *Trends in Migration Australia 2010–11:
     Annual Submission to OECD's Continuous Reporting System on Migration
     (SOPEMI)*, Department of Immigration and Citizenship,

Canberra, 2012, p. 51. According to the *Outlook for Net Overseas Migration* document, DIAC forecasts for the year ending 2012 a net overseas migration total of 192 600.

9   Julian Burnside, 'Remember our responsibility to protect refugees', *The Australian*, 2 September 2011, p. 14.

10 See Megalogenis, *The Australian Moment*, p. 118.

11 Kelly, *The March of Patriots*, p. 543.

12 Kelly, *The March of Patriots*.

13 Chandran Kukathas and William Maley, 'The Last Refuge: Hard and Soft Hansonism in Contemporary Australian Politics', CIS Issue Analysis No. 4, Centre for Independent Studies, Sydney, 1998.

14 Jim McKiernan 'The Political Imperative: Defend, Deter, Detain', in Mary Crock (ed.), *Protection or Punishment: The Detention of Asylum Seekers in Australia*, The Federation Press, Sydney, 1993.

15 Emma Griffiths, 'People smugglers should rot in hell: Rudd', ABC Radio National, *PM*, 17 April 2009, available at www.abc. net.au/pm/content/2008/s2546098.htm (last accessed 24 April 2012).

16 Fergus Hanson, *Australian and the World: Public Opinion and Foreign Policy*, The Lowy Institute Poll 2011, Lowy Institute for International Policy, Sydney, 2011, p. 14.

17 Suvendrini Perera, *Australia and the Insular Imagination: Beaches, Borders, Boats, and Bodies*, Palgrave Macmillan, New York, 2009, p. 165.

18 Robert Manne, *Making Trouble*, pp. 124–25.

19 David Hume, *Treatise of Human Nature: Being an Attempt to Introduce the Experimental Method of Reasoning into Moral Subjects*, [1739] 2006, available at http://ebooks.adelaide.edu.au/h/hume/david/h92t/ (last accessed 12 September 2011).

20 Adam Smith, *The Theory of Moral Sentiments*, Clarendon Press, Oxford, [1759] 1976.

21 Paul Sheehan, 'You call this even-handed? Refugee series is strictly for the gullible', *Sydney Morning Herald*, 23 June 2011, p. 17.

22 Greg Sheridan, 'ALP goes to water as boats threaten sovereignty', *The Australian*, 24 March 2011, p. 14.

23 Matthew Gibney, *The Ethics and Politics of Asylum: Liberal Democracy and the Response to Refugees*, Cambridge University Press, Cambridge, 2004, p. 229.

24 Department of Immigration and Citizenship, *Asylum Trends: Australia*, Department of Immigration and Citizenship, Canberra, 2011, p. 2.

25 Andy Lamey, *Frontier Justice: The Global Refugee Crisis and What to Do About It*, St Lucia, University of Queensland Press, 2011, p. 21.

26   Lamey, *Frontier Justice*, p. 171.

27   For examples of the universalist or cosmopolitan position, see
      Peter Singer and Renata Singer, 'The Ethics of Refugee Policy',
      in Mark Gibney (ed.), *Open Borders? Closed Societies?*, Greenwood
      Press, New York, 1998; and Kwame Anthony Appiah,
      Cosmopolitanism: Ethics in a World of Strangers, Allen Lane, London,
      2006.

28   Legrain, *Immigrants: Your Country Needs Them*, Ch. 1.

29   Christina Boswell, *The Ethics of Refugee Policy*, Ashgate Publishing,
      Aldershot, 2005, p. 1.

30   Walzer, *Spheres of Justice*, p. 31.

31   Hannah Arendt, *The Origins of Totalitarianism*, Allen & Unwin,
      London, 1967, pp. 299–300.

32   See Miller, *National Responsibility and Global Justice*, Oxford
      University Press, Oxford, 2007; Chok-Kor Tan, *Justice Without
      Borders: Cosmopolitanism, Nationalism and Patriotism*, Cambridge,
      Cambridge University Press, 2004.

33   Gibney, *Ethics and Politics of Asylum*, p. 84.

34   John Menadue, Arja Keski-Nummi and Kate Gauthier, *A New
      Approach: Breaking the Stalemate on Refugees and Asylum Seekers*, Centre
      for Policy Development, Sydney, 2011, p. 10.

35   Robert Manne, 'A two-step asylum seeker solution this
      government will not touch', ABC Online, *The Drum*, 12 April
      2011, available at www.abc.net.au/unleashed/55690.html (last
      accessed 12 September 2011).

36   See Menadue et al., *A New Approach*.

37   See Joint Select Committee on Australia's Immigration
      Detention Network, *Inquiry into Australia's Immigration Detention
      Network – Final Report*, Parliament House, Canberra, 2012,
      Ch. 5, available at www.aph.gov.au/Parliamentary_Business/
      Committees/Senate_Committees?url=immigration_detention_
      ctte/immigration_detention/index.htm (last accessed 26 April
      2012); see also Julian Burnside, 'What Do We Really Want from
      our Politicians?', *Canvass*, Vol. 2, September 2010, pp. 3–5,
      available at www.ethics.org.au/sites/default/files/Canvass%20
      Ethics%20of%20Asylum%20and%20Refugees%20October%20
      2011.pdf (last accessed 30 May 2012).

38   Joint Select Committee on Australia's Immigration Detention
      Network, *Inquiry into Australia's Immigration Detention Network*,
      pp. 19–23.

39   Milanda Rout and David Crowe, 'Morrison warns of "danger"
      to home-stay hosts', *The Australian*, 4 May 2012, p. 5; Scott
      Morrison, 'Labor's "Granny Flat" Solution is Desperate and
      Reckless', Media Release, 3 May 2012, available at
      www.scottmorrison.com.au/info/pressrelease.aspx?id=869 (last

accessed 1 June 2012).

40   Menadue et al., *A New Approach*, p. 13.

41   See Human Rights and Equal Opportunity Commission,
Immigration Detention and Offshore Processing on Christmas Island,
Human Rights and Equal Opportunity Commission, Sydney,
2009, available at www.hreoc.gov.au/human_rights/immigration/
idc2009_xmas_island.html#s8_1 (last accessed 12 September
2011).

42   *Plaintiff M70/2011 v Minister for Immigration and Citizenship; Plaintiff
M106 of 2011 v Minister for Immigration and Citizenship* [2011] HCA
32.

43   Menadue et al., *A New Approach*, p. 24.

44   At its most recent national conference in late 2011, the Labor
Party committed to increasing Australia's intake of refugees
progressive from 13 750 to 20 000 – on the condition that the
Gillard government's Malaysia Solution succeeds in reducing the
rate of boat arrivals: see Michael Gordon, 'Double or nothing on
refugee intake', *Sunday Age*, 4 December 2011, p. 5.

Afterword: Having a go

1   For a survey of language proficiency among humanitarian
entrants, see Australian Survey Research, *Settlement Outcomes
of New Arrivals – Report of Findings* (Study for Department of
Immigration and Citizenship), Ormond, Vic, 2011, pp. 12–17.

2   For an interesting example of this mercantilist language, see
Tim Lindsey, 'Australia's Asia literacy wipe-out', *The Interpreter*
(Lowy Institute for International Affairs blog), 4 November
2011, available at www.lowyinterpreter.org/post/2011/11/04/
Australias-Asia-literacy-wipe-out.aspx (last accessed 26 April
2012). While I don't disagree with the substance of Lindsey's
arguments, it is interesting that calls for greater Asian literacy,
even from a leading Asian scholar in Australia, were expressed in
such economistic language.

3   'And what should they know of England who only England
know?': Rudyard Kipling, 'The English Flag'.

4   For a recent discussion of language policy and multiculturalism
see Michael Clyne, 'Multilingualism, Multiculturalism and
Integration', in Clyne and Jupp (eds), *Multiculturalism and
Integration*. Cf. Joseph Lo Bianco, *National Policy on Languages*,
AGPS, Canberra, 1987; Department of Employment, Education,
and Training, *Australia's Language: The Australian Language and
Literacy Policy*, AGPS, Canberra, 1991.

5   Bob Carr, First Speech, Senate, 23 March 2012, available

at www.aph.gov.au/Senators_and_Members/Senators/First_
Speeches/First_Speeches/Bob_Carr_Senator_for_New_South_
Wales (last accessed 26 April 2012).

Index

population growth
Swan, Wayne 85

Tampa incident 39, 166–67, 172, 174
Tavan, Gwenda 14
Taylor, Charles 49–50, 94
Teo, Charlie 81
Thailand 175, 194, 195
The Boat 184
The Circuit 124
They're a Weird Mob 8
Thomson, Kelvin 161
Today Tonight 121
tolerance 14, 17, 21, 22, 30, 57, 67, 73, 76, 123
Trudeau, Pierre 9

Underbelly 118, 121

United States 9–10, 63, 64–66, 69, 139, 183

van Tongeren, Jack 23
Varganova, Elena 117
Vietnam 14, 164, 170

Walzer, Michael 162
Ward, Stuart 53–54
White Australia policy 7, 12, 16, 65, 80, 87, 118, 158
Whitlam, Gough 11, 12, 13, 15, 107

xenophobia *see* racism

Yang, Jerry 139